TENNESSEE

TENNESSEE BY ROAD

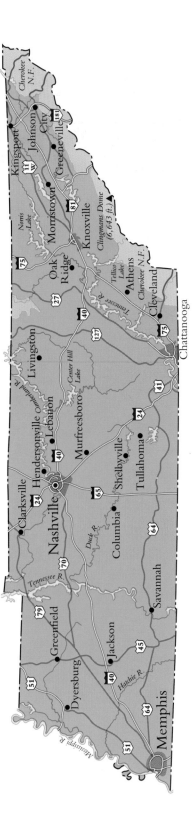

CELEBRATE THE STATES
TENNESSEE

Tracy Barrett

MARSHALL CAVENDISH
NEW YORK

For the seven-foot-tall Tennessee ridge runner

Benchmark Books
Marshall Cavendish Corporation
99 White Plains Road
Tarrytown, New York 10591-9001

Library of Congress Cataloging-in-Publication Data
Barrett, Tracy, date.
Tennessee / Tracy Barrett.
p.   cm. — (Celebrate the states ; 3)
Includes bibliographical references and index.
Summary: Surveys the geography, history, people, and customs of the state of Tennessee.
ISBN 0-7614-0208-X
1. Tennessee—Juvenile literature. [1. Tennessee.] I. Title. II. Series.
F436.3.B37   1998   976.8—dc21   96-44983   CIP   AC

Maps and graphics supplied by Oxford Cartographers, Oxford, England

Photo research by Ellen Barrett Dudley and Matthew J. Dudley

Cover photo: *Gary Layda* © 1996

The photographs in this book are used by permission and through the courtesy of: *The Image Bank*: Kathleen O'Donnell, 6-7; Edward Bower, 68, 73, 116, 125; Toby Rankin, 112; Andy Caulfield, 114 (left); Gary Cralle, 126. *Photo Researchers, Inc.*: Bruce Roberts, 10-11, 104; Kenneth Murray, 13, 18, 139; Frank J. Miller, 15; Jeff Greenberg, 20; Michael Hubrich, 22-23; Bonnie Sue, 76; Thomas S. England, 91, 114 (right); James Amos, 101, 102; H.H. Thornhill, 119 (left); Ray Coleman, 119 (right); Helen Williams, 122. *Bill Deane and the Department of Anthropology, University of Tennessee*: 17. *State of Tennessee, Photographic Services*: 16, 24, 61 (top and bottom), 67, 77, 79. *Metropolitan Museum of Art*: 26-27. *Tennessee State Museum*: 29, 37, 40, 55. *Corbis-Bettmann*: 31, 35, 41, 42, 52, 54, 83, 87, 128, 130, 132 (left and right), 133. *Woolaroc Museum, Bartlesville, Oklahoma*: 38. *AP/Wide World Photos*: 46. *UPI/Corbis- Bettmann*: 47, 85 (top), 96, 129, 135. *Gary Layda*: 48-49, 74, 107, 109, 110, 111, back cover. *TVA*: 57. *Ozark Yesteryear Photography*: 64-65, 80-81. *Raymond Bial*: 72, 98-99. *Reuters/Corbis-Bettmann*: 85 (bottom), 88 (top and bottom). *Springer/Corbis-Bettmann*: 90. *Cheekwood Museum of Art, Nashville, Tennessee*: 93. *Jim Carrol/Corbis-Bettmann*: 136.

Printed in Italy

1   3   5   6   4   2

CONTENTS

TENNESSEE IS . . .

The Great Smoky Mountains

Tennessee is beautiful country . . .

"The greenest state in the land of the free."
—theme song from 1950s television show *Davy Crockett*

"The fairest land
From God's own hand
Is the Basin of Tennessee."
—traditional song

"When civilization first peeped over the Alleghanies and looked down upon the gorgeous landscape below, I think she shouted . . . , Lo, this is Paradise regained!"
—Tennessee governor Robert L. Taylor, 1889

. . . with friendly people . . .

"Tennesseans may well be the most cussedly friendly people in the nation." —author Dana Facaros

"With his good-tempered easiness of manners, the Tennessean has a democratic feeling of equality. . . . His judgment and dignity proceed from himself." —from *Tennessee: A Guide to the State*, 1939

. . . who love their state.

"The Tennessee pioneer can be exceeded by none in fondness for
and admiration of his own country. . . . In all his wanderings, his
thoughts are turned constantly upon Tennessee."
—historian James G. M. Ramsey

"There's only one place worth living in, and that's Middle Tennessee. When I get out [of the military] . . . I'm going to marry a
Nashville gal. I'm going to buy some Middle Tennessee land and
raise Tennessee Walking Horses and Tennessee babies."
—homesick Tennessee soldier, 1960

"This is paradise. It's the most beautiful place I've ever seen."
—Tennessee newcomer Mary Bell

What is it about Tennessee that makes Tennesseans love their state
so deeply? Is it the natural beauty? . . . the dynamic and independent people? . . . the exciting things to do? Let's explore Tennessee
and find out!

1
THREE STATES
IN ONE

The three stars on the flag of Tennessee stand for the state's three grand divisions: east, middle, and west. These areas are so unlike one another that road signs on the state's borders used to say, "Welcome to the Three States of Tennessee."

These differences can be traced back to the forces that shape the land. Millions of years ago Tennessee was covered by ocean. Over millions of years, pieces of the earth's surface, called tectonic plates, rubbed against each other and rose up from the ocean. Their great ridges formed the Appalachian mountains, which run down the east coast of the United States from Canada to Georgia, through eastern Tennessee. The land to the west was not as disturbed by the collision of these great plates, so middle Tennessee is a land of gentle hills, while in the west the hills flatten out into wide plains.

Tennessee is shaped like a parallelogram. Only thirty-fourth of the fifty states in size, the state is almost four times as wide as it is high. If you were to stand in the northeastern corner of Tennessee, you would be closer to Canada than to the southwestern corner of the state!

Tennessee borders Kentucky and Virginia to the north; North Carolina to the east; Georgia, Alabama, and Mississippi to the south; and to the west, across the Mississippi River, Arkansas and Missouri. It stands at the crossroads of north and south, and of east and west.

Hikers in the Smokies often find fossils in the rocks.

Much of Tennessee is covered by forests of deciduous (hardwood) trees, such as oak, maple, beech, and walnut, which lose their leaves in a spectacular display of color each fall. In all parts of the state, small mammals such as opossums, raccoons, bobcats, foxes, and rabbits thrive. The largest wild animals left in Tennessee are black bears, white-tailed deer, and wild boars. Tennessee's 316 varieties of birds include most of those found in the rest of the United States, with quails, martens, and ravens especially common.

All of Tennessee is covered in flowers. One expert has said that there is "a larger number of flowers and ferns thriving in Tennessee than anywhere else in the world in an equal area."

EASTERN MOUNTAINS AND CAVES

The hills in the eastern third of Tennessee are so steep that roads have to wind among them rather than cut straight across. The Unaka Mountains, which make up the western edge of the Blue Ridge range of the Appalachians, cover east Tennessee. Most of Tennessee's 11,580 acres of forest lie in the east. These huge forests provide habitat for wildlife and, in the form of timber, income for the state.

Most of the rock under the mountains is limestone. Over time, limestone dissolves in water, and the many underground streams of the area have worn out some huge caves. More than seven thousand caves have been discovered in Tennessee, and about two hundred more are found every year.

In the southeastern corner of the state lies Lost Sea Caverns. This is the world's largest underground lake, covering four and one-half acres. Visitors can hike the three hundred feet down to the lake and ride in glass-bottomed boats to see the white trout and other unusual animals and rock formations.

East Tennessee's Cumberland Caverns, twenty-eight miles long, is the largest cave in the state and among the largest in the world. Early settlers excavated some rooms of the cave and made shelters in them. Humans weren't the only residents, though. Many contain jaguar and bear skeletons. Rats, beetles, and small

A farmer's fields in east Tennessee follow the contour of the rolling hills.

mammals such as raccoons still live there, as do many salamanders.

In the nineteenth century people who explored the cave often left their signatures on its walls and ceilings, writing them in the soot made by smoky torches. After the Civil War, the cave and the area around it became a popular picnicking spot.

Visitors take in the rock formations that seem to hover over the underground lake in Lost Sea Caverns, Sweetwater.

Today, people come from all over the country to explore the caves of Tennessee. "Caving isn't for everyone," says Greg Giles of Nashville. "It is dark and wet. There are many times when you have to lie down on your stomach and just inch along, and sometimes you even have to take off your helmet and push it in front of you and turn your head sideways so you can scoot through a very low place."

MUD GLYPH CAVE

In 1980, some amateur spelunkers, or cave explorers, asked a farmer's permission to explore the cave on his land. Another caver had told them that he had found strange markings, obviously made by humans, deep inside a cavern. This finding became known as Mud Glyph Cave (a glyph is a symbol that gives information without using words).

Many Indians thought of caves as sacred, holy places and explored deep into them to find rooms to use for religious ceremonies. They must have been brave indeed to go inside Mud Glyph Cave. After wiggling along flat against the ground through a passage called a belly-crawl, spelunkers hike along a stream, cold and dark and deep in the earth, before reaching a small room where the glyphs are found.

Anthropologists think that the glyphs were drawn between the twelfth and the eighteenth century. Some of them show no real shape but are squiggles drawn with all the fingertips of one hand. Others are pictures of animals—a snake, an owl, a hawk. There are also simple stick figures. One of these seems to be running, with its mouth open and arms thrown up in the air, as though in fear

West of the Unakas is the Great Valley of east Tennessee, a 9,200-square-mile segment of the Appalachian Mountain valley that runs from New York to central Alabama. The Great Valley is an agricultural center. Here tobacco, grain, and many fruits are grown, and cattle are raised.

In east Tennessee, the Appalachians rise so high that their climate is more like that of Canada than like the rest of the southern United States. Most of the trees are conifers, such as pines, that can survive in the cold. The Great Smoky Mountains in the Appalachians are covered with pines, and almost four thousand varieties of plants thrive here. One of the most spectacular is the wild tiger lily, which can grow to six feet high. The Smokies are filled with spectacular wild rhododendrons, which burst into red, pink, and white flowers in the spring. Roan Mountain has one rhododendron grove that spreads over more than six hundred acres!

THE MIDDLE: ROLLING HILLS AND PLAINS

When you have passed through the Great Valley and reached the Cumberland Plateau, you have arrived in middle Tennessee. Although you are fairly high up, the ground around you is almost as flat as a huge tabletop. This plateau is part of the Appalachian Highlands. The soil is too sandy for growing most crops, but the rivers and streams of the plateau are great for white-water rafting and canoeing.

Continuing west, you descend into the Central Basin, site of Nashville, the state's capital and largest city. This is a fertile area of gently rolling hills, where farmers used to grown cotton. Today, you are more likely to find grains, hay, and vegetables. The famous Tennessee walking horses graze in the large, fertile meadows.

The edge of the basin is called the Highland Rim. Tobacco and cotton are grown here, and minerals such as iron are mined. The beautiful hardwood forests supply oak, ash, hickory, and cedar for buildings and furniture.

Rhododendrons in their spectacular spring display

Children in farming families do their share of work.

WESTERN PLAINS AND SWAMPS

Even farther west, you'll find yourself in the Gulf Coastal Plain and the Flood Plains of the Mississippi River, where the heat, humidity, and flat land make cotton still a very important crop.

You'll also find Reelfoot, Tennessee's only natural lake of any size. The shallow waters of the lake have been called America's greatest natural fish hatchery. Not more than six to eight feet deep in any spot, Reelfoot is an ideal home for fish. This abundance of fish has attracted many waterbirds that feed on them, such as egrets,

THE BIRTH OF REELFOOT LAKE

Reelfoot, the only natural lake in Tennessee, was named for an Indian leader whose deformed foot caused him to walk crookedly, or reel. It was formed during a series of strong earthquakes in 1811 and 1812. The tremors could be felt for hundreds of miles and even made the churchbells ring in faraway Boston, Massachusetts!

The earth split open, and a deep depression was formed near the Mississippi River, which caused the mighty river to flow backward for about fifteen minutes, until it had filled the gully. When the river returned to its normal course, it left behind a wide, shallow lake.

Eliza Bryan, a newly arrived resident of the area, described the quake:

The Mississippi first seemed to recede from its banks, and its waters gathered up like a mountain, leaving for a moment many boats, which were on their way to New Orleans, on the bare sand, in which time the poor sailors made their escape from them.

Then rising 15 or 20 feet perpendicularly and expanding, as it were, at the same time, the banks overflowed with a retrograde current rapid as a torrent. The boats, which before had been left on the sand, were now torn from their moorings and suddenly driven up a little creek, . . . to a distance . . . of nearly a quarter of a mile.

herons, and anhingas. More than 250 kinds of birds live there or pass through.

Cypress trees thrive in the shallow water. The cypress has long, skinny roots that rise out of the water, forming a structure like a cage, with the trunk perched on top. These roots hold the tree upright in the mud at the bottom of the lake.

Western Tennessee is the site of the state's second-largest city, Memphis, and the lowest point in the state, rural Shelby County. The lowland often stays wet for long periods. Before modern medicine, the heat and humidity combined to make this an unhealthy area in which to live. In 1878, yellow fever, carried by swamp-loving mosquitoes, killed 5,152 people in Memphis.

Cypress trees in Reelfoot Lake's morning mist "look like they're wading up to their knees," says Margaret Jackson.

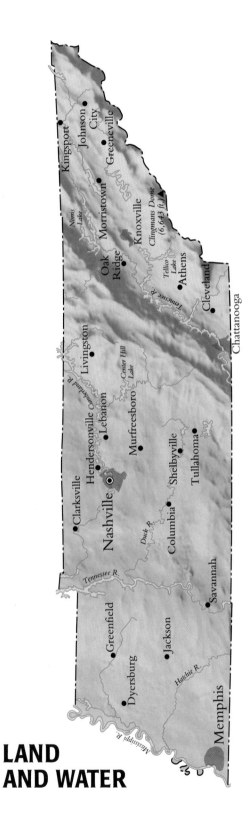

Kingsport

Johnson City

Greeneville

Morristown

Norris Lake

Knoxville

Clingmans Dome (6,643 ft.) ▲

Oak Ridge

Tellico Lake

Athens

Cleveland

Tennessee R.

Chattanooga

Livingston

Cumberland R.

Center Hill Lake

Hendersonville

Lebanon

Murfreesboro

Shelbyville

Tullahoma

Clarksville

Nashville

Duck R.

Columbia

Tennessee R.

Savannah

Greenfield

Jackson

Dyersburg

Hatchie R.

Memphis

Mississippi R.

LAND AND WATER

AN APPEALING BEAUTY

Since the Ice Age, Tennessee's beauty and comfortable climate have beckoned to settlers. The state has few extremes of heat or cold (the average temperature is 60 degrees Fahrenheit), although the mountainous east can have occasional hard winters and the steamy atmosphere around the Mississippi River makes the west uncomfortable in midsummer.

Boy Scouts' determination to leave an area cleaner than they found it has become a model for Tennessee's environmentalists.

Tennessee ranks in the bottom third of the states in area but seventeenth in population, with close to five million inhabitants and over three hundred incorporated cities. More than 60 percent of Tennesseans live in cities and towns of more than twenty-five hundred people. Many of these communities have colorful names, such as Bucksnort, Lovely City, Only, Red Boiling Springs, Stupidville, Frog Jump, Nosey Valley, and even Nameless.

Tennessee often ranks worst or second worst in air quality of all fifty states. In its eagerness to attract new business, the state legislature has refused to pass tough laws against pollution, and many of the beautiful streams of the east are among the most polluted in the country.

Tennesseans are strongly attached to their home state and increasingly aware of the damage that human activity causes to the environment. They began demanding more regulations in the 1980s and 1990s. Now new laws that protect the streams, wildlife, and air of Tennessee seek to undo some of that damage.

Tennesseans' loyalty to their beautiful state is the butt of an often-told joke. A newcomer to heaven asks, "Who are all those people chained to trees?" St. Peter replies, "Those are Tennesseans. It's Friday, and we have to chain them to keep them from going back home for the weekend."

2 A REMARKABLE HISTORY

Tennessee, by A. H. Wyant, 1866

Tennessee celebrated its two hundredth birthday as a state on June 1, 1996, but the history of people in Tennessee starts more than eleven thousand years ago. That was when the first Indians entered the region in pursuit of mastodons and other game animals as glaciers melted at the end of the Ice Age.

The early Indians left behind some mysterious remains: large mounds in which they buried their dead. One of the largest is Old Stone Fort, near Manchester in south-central Tennessee. This massive construction has dirt walls twenty feet thick, covered with stone. Pinson Mound, more than seventy feet high, is the second-tallest Indian mound in the United States.

When the first European settlers arrived in Tennessee in the sixteenth century, about ten thousand Indians were living there. The major tribes were the Creeks, Shawnee, Yuchi, and most numerous of all, the Cherokee, who called themselves Ani-Yunwiya, the Real People.

In the early 1700s, the Cherokees, who were ferocious fighters, forced the Creeks and Yuchis out of east Tennessee. Some Yuchi warriors, trapped on the banks of the Hiwassee River in east Tennessee, were so terrified of being captured by the Cherokees that they massacred their people and committed suicide rather than fall into the hands of their enemies. By the mid-1700s, the Cherokees were the only tribe left in Tennessee, with about

Some early European settlers thought that a twelfth-century Welsh prince built these enormous Indian mounds.

twenty-two thousand people living in eighty towns.

In every town was a main council house where the tribal leaders met for religious and official functions. Often this house was large enough to seat five hundred people. Each tribe was divided into seven clans (groups of people who are related to one another). The council houses had seven sides so that each of the clans could be seated together.

Cherokee society was matrilineal, meaning that children

THE RABBIT AND THE TAR WOLF: A CHEROKEE TALE

Once there was such a long spell of dry weather that there was no more water in the creeks and springs. The animals held a council to see what to do about it. They decided to dig a well and all agreed to help, except the Rabbit, who was a lazy fellow and said, "I don't need to dig for water. The dew on the grass is enough for me."

The others did not like this, but they went to work together and dug their well. They noticed that the Rabbit kept sleek and lively, although it was still dry weather and the water was getting low in the well. They said, "That tricky Rabbit steals our water at night."

So they made a wolf of pine gum and tar and set it up by the well to scare the thief. That night the Rabbit came, as he had been coming every night, to drink enough to last him all the next day. He saw the queer black thing by the well and said, "Who's there?"

The tar wolf said nothing. The Rabbit came nearer, but the wolf never moved. So the Rabbit grew braver and said, "Get out of my way, or I'll strike you." Still the wolf never moved—and the Rabbit came up and struck it with his paw. The gum held his foot and it stuck fast.

Now the Rabbit was angry and said, "Let me go, or I'll kick you." Still the wolf said nothing. Then the Rabbit struck again with his hind foot so hard that it was caught in the gum and he could not move. And there he stuck until the animals came for water in the morning. When they found who the thief was they had great sport over him for a while and then got ready to kill him. One proposed cutting his head off. This the Rabbit said would be useless, because it had been tried before without hurting him. Other methods were proposed for killing him, all of which he said would be useless. At last, it was proposed to let him loose to perish in a thicket. Upon this the Rabbit pretended great uneasiness, and he pled hard for his life. His enemies, however, refused to listen, and he was let loose in the thicket. As soon as he was out of reach, he gave a whoop and bounding away, he exclaimed, "This is where I live!"

belonged to their mother's clan. Before the arrival of the white settlers, some of the most important Cherokee leaders were women.

FRONTIER WILDERNESS

The first Europeans to set foot in Tennessee were Spanish. In 1540, the explorer Hernando de Soto called the area around the Tennessee River "a wilderness, having many pondy places, with thick forests [and] some basins and lakes." English and French explorers soon followed.

Spanish explorer Hernando de Soto entered Tennessee in 1540. He reached the shores of the Mississippi River in spring of the following year.

The Europeans were delighted with what they found. The land was beautiful and fertile, and the woods and fields were full of bison and elk. But there were difficulties, too. Wolves and cougars preyed on precious livestock. Most of the Cherokees were furious about the invasion of the land.

One leader who tried to keep settlers away was Tsu-gun-sini (Dragging Canoe). He was bitterly opposed to the white settlements in Tennessee and refused to sign treaties with white people. His Chickamauga warriors fiercely attacked the earliest settlers.

Yet white explorers continued to come. John William Gerhard de Brahm said in 1756: "Should this country once come into the hands of the Europeans, they may with propriety call it the American Canaan [Paradise]." But only the hardiest could bear the rugged frontier life. The early trail blazers earned the name "long hunters," since they survived such a long time in the wilderness.

What brought settlers to Tennessee? Some were looking for a passage westward across the Appalachians. This was found in 1775, when long hunter Daniel Boone located the Cumberland Gap. An entry in the journal of explorer Pierre de Charlevoix's journal of 1721 reads, "The country is delightful. . . . As to the forests, which almost entirely cover this immense country, there is, perhaps, nothing in nature comparable to them."

The majority of Europeans came to the area to build a new and free life. The first city in Tennessee was Jonesborough, founded in 1779 in the eastern part of the state. Fort Nashborough, later called Nashville, was established that same winter by James Robertson and John Donelson. The settlement grew slowly. Lewis Brantz's 1785 journal noted that "Nashville is a recently founded place and contains only two houses . . . the rest are only huts."

Most settlers lived in log cabins of just one room, with wooden floors. Travel was difficult. Francis Baily, an Englishman who visited Tennessee in the 1790s, said of a tavern, "There were three or four beds of the roughest construction in one room, which was open at all hours of the night for the reception of any rude rabble that had a mind to put up at the house; and if the other beds happened to be occupied, you might be surprised when you awoke in the morning to find a bed fellow by your side whom you had never seen before, and might never see again."

POPULATION GROWTH: 1790–1990

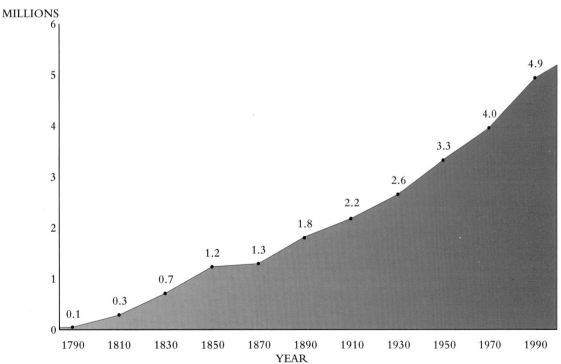

CUMBERLAND GAP

Cumberland Mountain is part of the Appalachian Mountain Range, which extends from Pennsylvania to Alabama. The Cumberland Gap, located where Tennessee, Virginia, and Kentucky meet, is a deep pass in the mountain that served as one of the main pathways by which the early settlers were able to move westward. Daniel Boone, noted backwoodsman, trapper, and Indian fighter, came upon the Gap in 1775.

The first white man in Cumberland Gap,
The first white man in Cumberland Gap,
The first white man in Cumberland Gap,
Was Doctor Walker, an English chap.

Daniel Boone on Pinnacle Rock,
Daniel Boone on Pinnacle Rock,
Daniel Boone on Pinnacle Rock,
He killed bears with his old flintlock.

Cumberland Gap is a noted place,
Cumberland Gap is a noted place,
Cumberland Gap is a noted place,
Three kinds of water to wash your face.

Cumberland Gap, with its cliffs and rocks,
Cumberland Gap, with its cliffs and rocks,
Cumberland Gap, with its cliffs and rocks,
Home of the panther, bear, and fox.

Me and my wife and my wife's grandpap,
Me and my wife and my wife's grandpap,
Me and my wife and my wife's grandpap,
We all live in Cumberland Gap.

Daniel Boone leads a party of early settlers west across the Appalachians through the Cumberland Gap.

Near Norris in east Tennessee is the Museum of Appalachia, one of the world's largest and most authentic historic parks, which is dedicated to representing the early history of the settlers in Tennessee. Here visitors can see twenty-five reconstructed log cabins and many artifacts from the hills: farm implements, household items, and toys. Local people demonstrate crafts common to the region, such as basket weaving and whittling.

THE PATH TO STATEHOOD

The American colonies declared their independence from Great Britain in 1776. The Revolutionary War was fought to defend this independence. Though Tennessee was not a colony, its residents took action when the British tried to take control of the "over-mountain" territories, which included what is now Tennessee. One thousand Tennesseans went to fight with the Americans in South Carolina. They helped win one of the war's most important conflicts, the Battle of King's Mountain, in 1780.

After the Revolution, Tennessee became part of North Carolina. Then in 1784, the independent East Tennesseans broke away and formed a new country, the Republic of Franklin (named for Benjamin Franklin). They elected John Sevier governor; but after his term ended, no one else was interested in governing the "country." So in 1788, Franklin rejoined North Carolina.

A year later, Tennessee became the "Territory South of the River Ohio." Most residents were happy when in 1796 the population reached eighty thousand, which was enough for statehood. Tennessee was made the sixteenth state, the first state created from

At the end of the Battle of King's Mountain, all one thousand British soldiers were killed, wounded, or captured, while of the nine hundred Americans, twenty-eight were killed and sixty-two wounded.

a territory. Knoxville was its capital, and the popular John Sevier became its first governor.

THE TRAIL OF TEARS

In 1812, the United States once again went to war with England. So many Tennesseans volunteered to fight that the state earned the nickname Volunteer State. Tennessee's Andrew Jackson became one of the greatest heroes of the War of 1812. He would go on to be elected president of the United States in 1828 and again in 1832.

Jackson acted ruthlessly against the Indians, both as a soldier and as president. Davy Crockett, who fought with Jackson, later said that under Jackson's command the Indians were shot "like dogs."

It was Jackson who ordered that the Cherokees be removed west of the Mississippi River. Some of the Tennessee Cherokees managed to hide from the soldiers who were rounding them up, and their descendants now live in east Tennessee. The white people called this forced march in the harsh winter of 1838–1839 "The Indian Removal," but it is better known today by the Cherokee name: The Trail of Tears.

More than four thousand Cherokees died during the forced removal from their homeland. They called their journey nuna da ut sun y, *"the place where they cried."*

Many Indians as well as white people fought in vain to prevent this brutal action. A general who was ordered to force the Cherokees off their lands told his soldiers to disobey, saying he refused to carry out "at the point of the bayonet a treaty made by a lean minority against the will and authority of the Cherokee people."

But Jackson's will ultimately won out. The Indians slowly made their way across the country, traveling on foot and by flatboat. One observer to their passage saw in their faces "a downcast defeated look bordering upon the appearance of despair." Of the 17,000 Indians forced to leave their ancestral lands, about 4,000 had died by the time the Cherokees reached their final destination in Oklahoma.

FROM SLAVERY TO CIVIL WAR

Meanwhile, most black Tennesseans lived in slavery. In the early nineteenth century, some white people, especially in the eastern part of the state, formed societies to free slaves, but most of them had given up by the 1830s. A constitutional convention of 1834 took away free blacks' right to vote (slaves had never had it). In 1840, 183,057 Tennesseans were slaves, and only about 5,000 blacks were free.

Disagreements over the rights of states to decide certain matters, among the most important the legality of slavery, led eleven southern states to secede (remove themselves) from the United States. The people of Tennessee had a hard time agreeing on whether to secede. It has been said that "Tennessee's head was with the Union, but her heart was with the South." When the Civil War broke out, the state joined the Confederacy. Scott County, in

Slaves are sold in Nashville in full view of Tennessee's capitol—a symbol of democracy.

pro-Union east Tennessee, promptly seceded from Tennessee and did not officially rejoin the state until 1986.

More Civil War battles were fought in Tennessee than in any other state except Virginia. The bloodiest combat of the entire war took place at the west Tennessee town of Shiloh in 1862, where 23,500 men were killed. The Battle of Shiloh shocked the nation. In this one conflict, more soldiers were killed than in all three wars that had been fought on American soil before that day (the Revolution, the War of 1812, and the Mexican War).

The peaceful fields erupted in smoke and the crack of rifles. Children who went out to play in the morning could not make their way home through the bloodshed. When they did, they found a path covered with dead and dying soldiers, their farmhouses destroyed, and their families either dead or in flight from the marauding armies.

Carol Hamlett, who grew up in nearby Crockett County, says of the battlefield, "For anyone who has any sense of history, the place is so peaceful, yet so somber. It's all still there. There isn't any big city nearby to take over the land, so you can still see the fields and orchards the way they were when the battle was being fought."

Twenty thousand black Tennesseans fought in the Civil War, most of them on the Union side. In the last important conflict in

Southerners still refer to this horrifying battle as "bloody Shiloh."

Slaves flocked to join the Union Army when they were promised their freedom in exchange for enlisting.

the state, the Battle of Nashville (December 1864), more than 15 percent of the soldiers in the front lines were black. "The blood of white and black men has flowed freely together," said Union general George Thomas, "for the great cause which is to give freedom."

The Civil War divided Tennessee as it did no other state. About 100,000 to 135,000 of its citizens fought for the Confederacy, against 55,000 to 70,000 for the Union. When the war was over, Tennessee, the last state to join the Confederacy, was the first to rejoin the Union.

A GIRL WITH A MISSION

Most Americans know about Paul Revere, who rode twelve miles to warn the colonists that the redcoats were coming at the start of the American Revolution. But how many have heard that Tennessee teenager Mary Love rode thirty-five miles through enemy territory on an equally dangerous mission in the Civil War?

Union general Ulysses S. Grant needed to send a message to General Ambrose Burnside in Knoxville. So risky was this mission that he sent five different messengers by five different routes, hoping that at least one of them would make it. When one courier stopped, exhausted, at the Love home in Kingston, Mary hid the message in her clothes, leaped on a horse, and galloped off toward Knoxville.

She was caught by the enemy and taken in for questioning but did not give any information—unlike Paul Revere! They released her, and she continued on to her brother's home in Knoxville, arriving there too exhausted to finish the journey. A thirteen-year-old boy took the message the rest of the way.

The war shattered the state. A visitor said in 1863, "In happier days, Nashville must have been a very pleasant dwelling-place; but when I saw it, the whole aspect of the city was, even for a stranger, a dreary and dismal one. . . . [It looked] like a city still stunned by the blow of some great public calamity."

REBUILDING

The end of the Civil War did not mean the end of racial troubles in Tennessee. In 1866, the Ku Klux Klan, a fiercely white supremacist group, was formed in Pulaski, Tennessee. One of its earliest leaders was former Confederate general Nathan Bedford Forrest. Forrest had been a slave trader in Memphis before becoming a soldier. The Klan tried to keep blacks from voting (a right they won in 1867) and from assuming other civil rights. The Klan was outlawed in 1869.

Reconstruction (the post-Civil War era) was very hard on Tennessee. The economy was ruined. Most of the farms had been burned. The North was bitter toward its former enemy, and much of the South did not trust the state that had been drawn so reluctantly into the Confederacy.

Still, the state began slowly to rebuild itself. Tennesseans realized the importance of education in helping their state rebound from the disastrous war. School reforms began immediately after the Civil War. A public school system for whites was established in 1867, although separate public schools for black children did not open until 1909. Fisk, a black university, was founded in 1866 in a former Union Army hospital. And in 1873, New York millionaire Cornelius Vanderbilt gave $1 million to Vanderbilt University to help the healing process between North and South.

STRUGGLING FOR EQUAL RIGHTS

One of the bitterest fights in early twentieth-century America was the battle over votes for women. In order for women to gain this right, the United States Constitution had to be amended, or changed. Thirty-six states had to ratify (approve) this amendment for it to become law. By a narrow majority, in 1920 Tennessee became the thirty-sixth state to ratify the amendment. Unfortunately, it sometimes seems as if this battle was fought to little purpose. Today, few women of Tennessee turn out to vote. Campaigns to encourage women to go to the polls, such as Women Rock the Vote, seemed to have little impact in 1996: A smaller percentage of women in Tennessee voted in the national election than in any other state in the country.

Another intense conflict in this century has been the struggle for racial equality. In 1890, many of the rights blacks had won in the Civil War and Reconstruction eras were taken away from them. The Ku Klux Klan was revived, and its members terrorized and killed blacks to prevent them from fighting for equal rights. Blacks suspected of offenses as small as being rude to a white person were lynched—attacked by a mob and killed. Their bodies were sometimes left hanging in public places to frighten others. Between 1880 and 1950, approximately two hundred black Tennesseans were lynched. New "Jim Crow" laws separated the races on buses, in schools, and even in parks.

In 1954, the United States Supreme Court ordered school integration. By signing a paper called the Southern Manifesto, many southern senators defied this law. Tennessee senator Estes Kefauver's refusal to sign it made him many enemies. School integration began in most of Tennessee in 1956, although Memphis did not integrate until 1961. Ellen Smith was a girl when the Nashville schools were integrated. "There were lots of demonstrations against integration downtown," she recalls. "People were furious. I remember worrying that our housekeeper wouldn't like us anymore because we were white. But she never mentioned the riots to me."

Blacks' voting rights were restored in the 1960s. It did not take long for blacks to start making their mark in Tennessee politics. In 1964, A. W. Willis became the first black elected to the Tennessee legislature. But it took more than thirty years before Tennessee had a black chief justice of the state Supreme Court, A. A. Birch Jr., in 1996.

Civil rights leader Dr. Martin Luther King Jr., who had won a

Their smiling faces contrasting with their hate-filled signs, white high-school students protest the end of segregation.

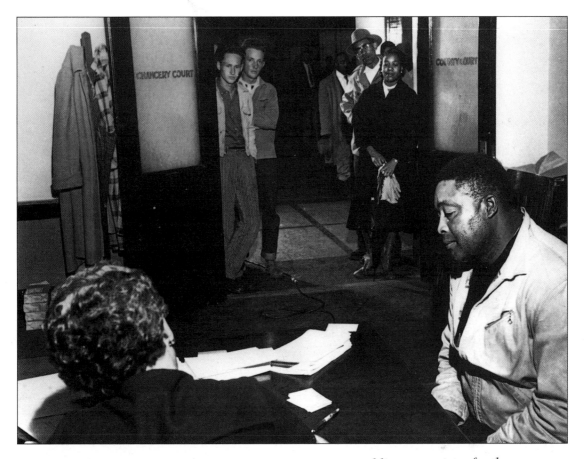

In Somerville, west Tennessee, voters wait in segregated lines to register for the 1960 primaries.

Nobel Peace Prize for his nonviolent crusade for equal rights, went to Memphis in 1968 to try to help the sanitation workers who were on strike. In one of the most tragic episodes of American history, King was assassinated there, and today a civil rights museum stands on the spot where he was killed.

Tennesseans have fought long and hard to get where they are today. As President Theodore Roosevelt put it, "No state has a more remarkable and romantic history than Tennessee."

3 BEYOND WATAUGA

Tennessee's capitol in Nashville with equestrian statue of Andrew Jackson

In 1772, a band of settlers in east Tennessee organized themselves into a group called the Watauga Association. They were led by James Robertson and John Sevier, who later became Tennessee's first governor. The members of the Watauga Association wrote the Articles, the first written constitution in America.

Since many of Tennessee's settlers had gone to the new territory to escape colonial government, they resented this new control. Most of these independent-minded people settled in the remote eastern hills, far from government of any kind. Today, the residents of east Tennessee still have a reputation for disliking government and preferring to settle their problems among themselves, without what they call "interference" from the authorities.

But most Tennesseans recognize the need for a state government. Tennessee's first constitution was approved when it became a state in 1796. A new one was approved in 1834, and a third in 1870. This latter document, with several amendments, is the one in force in Tennessee today.

INSIDE GOVERNMENT

Like the nation itself and most states, Tennessee has three branches of government: the legislative, the executive, and the judicial.

Legislative. Tennessee's legislative branch is responsible for

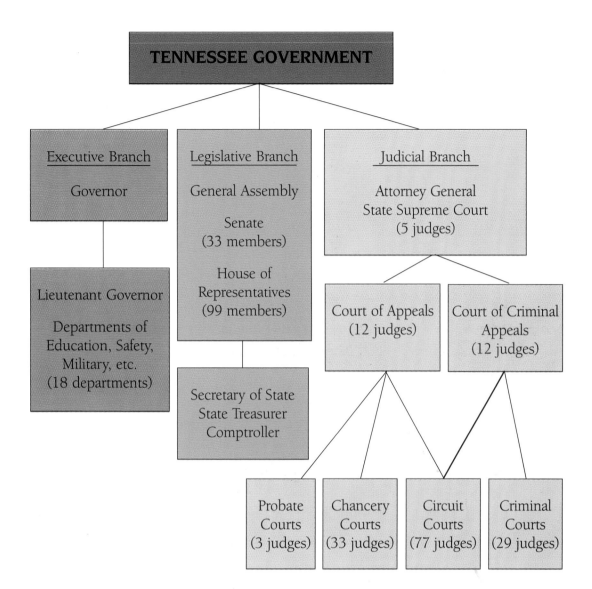

TENNESSEE GOVERNMENT

Executive Branch

Governor

Lieutenant Governor

Departments of
Education, Safety,
Military, etc.
(18 departments)

Legislative Branch

General Assembly

Senate
(33 members)

House of
Representatives
(99 members)

Secretary of State
State Treasurer
Comptroller

Judicial Branch

Attorney General
State Supreme Court
(5 judges)

Court of Appeals
(12 judges)

Court of Criminal
Appeals
(12 judges)

Probate
Courts
(3 judges)

Chancery
Courts
(33 judges)

Circuit
Courts
(77 judges)

Criminal
Courts
(29 judges)

making the laws for the state. The legislature, called the General
Assembly, contains two bodies: the senate, with thirty-three members, and the house of representatives, with ninety-nine. The
members of the General Assembly are elected by the communities
they live in and represent.

Two presidents of the United States, James K. Polk and Andrew

David Crockett never wore a raccoon-skin cap, despite his image as a rough-and-ready frontiersman.

Jackson, began their political careers as Tennessee state legislators. David (Davy) Crockett, the nineteenth-century frontiersman who later became a U.S. congressman and then died at the Alamo in Texas, was a Tennessee legislator, as was Cordell Hull, the longest-serving United States secretary of state.

Executive. The executive branch of Tennessee's government is headed by the governor. Most governors have been Democrats—since 1893, there have been only five Republican governors of Tennessee. The governor recommends new laws to the General Assembly. If the assembly passes a law that the governor does not approve of, he (all of Tennessee's governors have been men) may veto, or cancel, it. The governor is the head of the state militia (army). The governor also appoints the judges and the commissioners who head the various departments.

Judicial. The state courts and the judges who preside over them make up the judicial branch of the government. Tennessee's judicial system has been criticized for being unnecessarily complicated. There are four levels of courts. The highest is the state supreme court. Below it are the intermediate appellate courts, then the four courts (probate, criminal, circuit, and chancery) that make up the trial courts. At the lowest level are the courts of limited jurisdiction, such as the juvenile courts.

In some counties, the judges are elected by the people. In others, they are appointed by the mayor. What kinds of cases the different courts rule on also varies from county to county. Some crimes are covered by more than one court, making it difficult to decide who should conduct the trial. Sometimes it takes an expert lawyer just to figure out which court should hear a particular case. Occasional attempts have been made to reform the system, so far without success.

PROMINENT POLITICIANS

Many Tennesseans have served with distinction in the federal government, three of them as president: Andrew Jackson (1829–1837), James K. Polk (1845–1849), and Andrew Johnson (1865–1869).

Andrew Jackson was the first American president from west of the

THE MONKEY TRIAL

One of the most famous legal battles in American history, the Scopes trial, or "Monkey Trial," took place in Dayton, Tennessee, in 1925. Tennessee had outlawed the teaching of evolution, making it illegal for any teacher to "teach any theory that denies the story of the Divine Creation of man as taught in the Bible, and to teach instead that man has descended from a lower order of animals." A teacher named John Thomas Scopes thought that this law was wrong and deliberately broke it to force a court to hear the case. Scopes lost his case (although he was never sent to prison). Evolution was not legally taught in Tennessee until 1967.

History almost repeated itself in 1995 when the Tennessee legislature tried to pass a new law requiring evolution to be taught as theory, not fact. The bill was defeated.

James K. Polk campaigning in 1840 in Knoxville. Artist unknown.

Appalachians. All earlier presidents were from wealthy families, but Jackson was born in a log cabin and grew up on the frontier. His father died a few days before he was born, and he lost his mother when he was fourteen. Jackson fought at least two duels, killing his opponent in one of them. His toughness earned him the nickname Old Hickory. A famous soldier, Jackson was very popular during his presidency, especially with people in the western United States.

In the 1840s, Tennessee grew in both size and importance. Governor James K. Polk was elected U.S. president in 1844, even though his own state did not vote for him. The Mexican War was fought during Polk's presidency. His fellow Tennesseans rallied to their president, and thirty thousand of them volunteered for military service.

Tennessee senator Andrew Johnson had remained loyal to the Union before and during the Civil War and was the only southern senator to speak up against secession. He was elected vice president in 1864 and became president in 1865 when Lincoln was assassinated. The northerners thought he, a southerner, was being too easy on the south. Southerners, on the other hand, could not forgive his siding with the Union. He was impeached (brought to trial) in 1868 and was acquitted by just one vote.

Cordell Hull served as U.S. secretary of state during World War II and became one of the organizers of the United Nations. He won the Nobel Peace Prize in 1945.

Senator Howard Baker, from Huntsville, Tennessee, was the Senate minority leader and then majority leader during much of the 1970s and 1980s. He was one of the leaders of the committee that investigated the Watergate affair when President Richard Nixon was suspected of committing crimes in his effort to be reelected president. Baker also served as President Ronald Reagan's chief of staff.

Lamar Alexander was Tennessee's governor from 1978 to 1987, then served as secretary of education under President George Bush. He ran unsuccessfully for the Republican presidential nomination in 1996.

THE TENNESSEE VALLEY AUTHORITY

Tennesseans are in general poorer than most other Americans. In 1994, Tennessee ranked twenty-eighth of the fifty states in the average income of its residents. This is an improvement over 1980, when it was in forty-first place. And in 1996, Tennessee led the nation in job and income gains.

These gains represent a vast improvement since 1929, the first year of the Great Depression, which plunged much of the country into unemployment and poverty. The Depression hit Tennessee hard. The whole country suffered, but the Southeast was worse off than other regions: The average income of a Tennessean in 1929 was only about half that of the country as a whole.

To help the state and the region, the federal government started a program called the Tennessee Valley Authority, or TVA, in 1933.

In 1933, families in rural Tennessee were still living the way their ancestors had centuries before.

The TVA built dams on the Tennessee River and its tributaries. These dams brought electricity for the first time to parts of Tennessee. They also controlled floods and created lakes. Some Tennesseans were opposed to the dams, especially when their homes were flooded by the resulting lakes. Although they were paid for their property, many had to be forcibly removed by federal agents.

Today, the TVA operates thirty-five dams. Other federal programs, such as the Civilian Conservation Corps (CCC), employed out-of-work Tennesseans in construction projects. "They did a lot of things for the people in the state," says Greg Giles. "The park shelters built by the CCC are wonderful. But you have to have mixed feelings about the TVA. A lot of people in Tennessee might still be without electricity if the TVA hadn't come in, but they disrupted a lot of people's lives by flooding their homes."

EDUCATION

Lack of education among Tennesseans has hurt the state's economy. Nineteenth-century philanthropist George Peabody, a northerner, gave the state money to support the public schools. Even so, in 1900, fewer than half of Tennessee's children attended school. Although that number has risen dramatically, in 1990 almost one-third of Tennesseans aged twenty-five and older had not graduated from high school. Teachers' salaries are below the national average, and the state ranks last or close to last in the amount of money spent on public education.

School integration was resisted in much of the state until the federal government stepped in. Today, Nashville is considered by some a national model of school integration, although some residents, both black and white, think that the money spent on busing should be put directly into the schools themselves. Education in the state continues to improve, with about half of every tax dollar going to fund public schools. In 1996, Tennessee became the first state in the nation to have every public school linked to the Internet.

ECONOMIC STRIDES

Besides improved education, Tennesseans' lives are getting better in other ways. Exports are growing, as is the state's economy as a whole.

1992 GROSS STATE PRODUCT: $108.9 BILLION

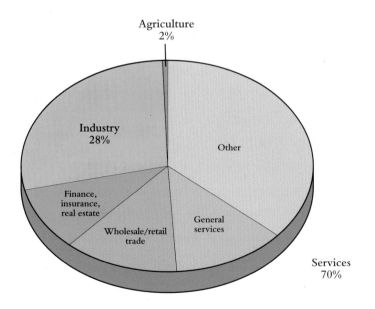

Agriculture
2%

Industry
28%

Other

Finance,
insurance,
real estate

Wholesale/retail
trade

General
services

Services
70%

The employment rate is now higher than the national average.

The first factories in Tennessee were built in the 1880s. They were mostly textile mills. Manufacturing boomed in the state in the 1950s and 1960s. Today, manufacturing accounts for nearly one-third of the state's economy and employs about half a million Tennesseans. Clothing, chemicals, food, industrial machines, and transportation equipment are the most important industries.

The automobile industry is also growing. Before World War I, a car called the Marathon was made in Tennessee, but it never became popular, and the factory shut down after a few years. Car manufacturing returned to the state in 1982 when Nissan opened its plant in Smyrna. Today, it is the largest single automobile factory in the United States. General Motors' Saturn plant in Spring Hill is considered a model of a worker-friendly environment. Tennessee is now the fifth-largest auto-manufacturing state in the United States.

Farming has declined as a source of income in Tennessee since the nineteenth century, but it is still important, especially in the middle and western parts of the state. Soybeans, tobacco, cotton, wheat, and corn are the most important crops. Unfortunately, much of the land is overfarmed, making it hard to produce as many crops in a small area as farmers used to grow. The Farm Bill of 1985 is an attempt to halt erosion. It suggests that farmers rotate crops (plant different things in fields at different times) and plant trees on worn-out cropland to keep the soil from wearing away.

Great strides have been made in improving the economy of Tennessee. But the state's residents still disagree over the best way to attract new business. Some want to weaken the already feeble

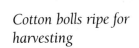

Cotton bolls ripe for harvesting

Despite opposition by antismoking forces, tobacco remains an important source of income for many Tennessee families.

EARNING A LIVING

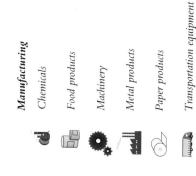

Agriculture

- 🌽 Corn
- Cotton
- 🐖 Hogs
- Sheep
- Soybeans
- Tobacco

Natural Resources

- **BC** Ball clay
- Coal
- **L** Limestone
- **M** Marble
- **Ph** Phosphate rock
- **Zn** Zinc

Manufacturing

- Chemicals
- Food products
- Machinery
- Metal products
- Paper products
- Transportation equipment

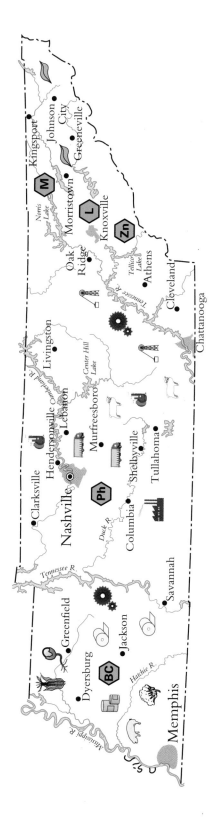

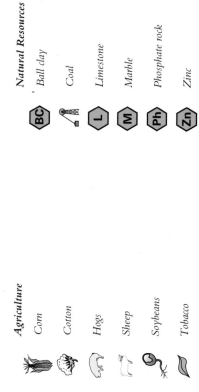

environmental laws to make it less expensive for manufacturers to operate in Tennessee. Others argue that the state's natural beauty is one of its most precious assets and will by itself draw new businesses into the area. Some say that spending money on education will make Tennesseans more productive workers and will encourage more people to move to the state, while others say that tax money would be better spent in building factories and giving tax breaks to new businesses.

4 WOVEN FROM A SINGLE THREAD

Fiddler, Museum of Appalachia, Norris

Who are Tennesseans? Where did their ancestors come from? Today, the traditional three-part division of the state holds less true when talking about the people than about the geography. In the past, though, people were more tied to the land, so geographic differences led to different ways of life.

East Tennessee consisted mostly of small farms and tiny isolated communities. This was due to the independent spirit of the people who lived there, as well as to the difficulty of travel in the hills in the days before interstate highways. And the hilly, rocky terrain of east Tennessee did not lend itself to large plantations, so the area had very few slaves.

Most settlers of middle and west Tennessee, the flatter parts of the state, immigrated from Virginia and North Carolina. They brought slaves and the plantation setup with them. Farms in the middle and west thus tended to be bigger than in the east. Large numbers of people, both slave and free, worked the land. In the west, cattle and horses grazed in the fields, while farmers in the east tended to raise hardier, smaller animals (such as pigs and goats) that could graze on hills.

The immigrants from North Carolina and Virginia also brought many customs with them. Among these was the practice of laying out a town with a common town square or green and a community church. This, combined with the greater ease of travel in the middle

Pumpkins and other crops thrive in the fertile Tennessee soil.

Tennessee hills and the west Tennessee flatlands, made for the growth of larger communities in these areas.

Although most people in the hills work in cities and towns today, the past still shapes people's lives. Carol Hamlett's great-great-great-grandfather moved from North Carolina to west Tennessee's Crockett County in 1843. His cotton farm prospered, and Carol grew up in the large house he had built. Her family still farmed cotton when she was a child, but by the 1950s a series of regula-

Beautiful Spring Hill is being transformed as industry moves into the area.

tions limited the amount of cotton any one farm could produce, so they moved off the land.

Carol says, "Once the cotton allotment laws were passed, it was hard for people to make a living in west Tennessee. When you go there, it's like stepping back in time. This is part of the charm of the area, but it's also depressing—things haven't changed because people don't have the jobs and the money to make a change."

ETHNIC TENNESSEE

Almost all Tennesseans—99 percent—were born in the United States. The number of Tennesseans born in their native state is also much higher than the national average. Now the numbers of immigrants are beginning to increase. Tennessee's projected 1995 population showed 4,327,000 white residents, 845,000 black, 46,000 Asian, and 11,000 Indian. The Hispanic population, although growing too, is still small. Recently the state has seen an increasing number of Japanese immigrants. Meiji Gakuin is the first fully accredited Japanese high school in the United States. These new Tennesseans have brought different religions, traditions, arts, foods, stories, and games to the state.

In general, more Tennessean blacks live in cities than in rural areas. Nashville's estimated 1995 population of 1,070,000 is about 24 percent black, while the Memphis area, with about 1,056,000 people, is almost 55 percent black. The cities in general have shown a decline in black population since the 1950s, when many black people migrated from the South to seek work in the cities of the North.

ETHNIC TENNESSEE

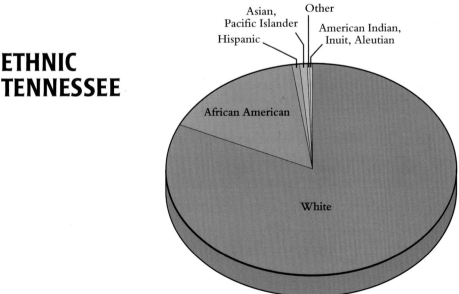

TEN LARGEST CITIES

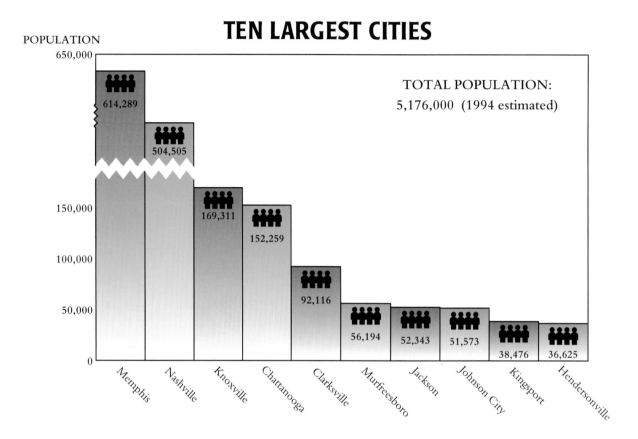

POPULATION

TOTAL POPULATION:
5,176,000 (1994 estimated)

650,000

614,289

504,505

150,000

169,311

152,259

100,000

92,116

50,000

56,194

52,343

51,573

38,476

36,625

0

Memphis
Nashville
Knoxville
Chattanooga
Clarksville
Murfreesboro
Jackson
Johnson City
Kingsport
Hendersonville

THE BUCKLE ON THE BIBLE BELT

"Before the arrival of the settlers," says Tennessean Allison Shaw, who is half Native American, "the Indians lived like kings and queens of the land." The rich religious and spiritual lives of the Cherokees and other tribes were a vital part of their cultures. Many of their traditional beliefs and practices were destroyed by the disruption of their way of life when the white settlers moved in. By the time of the Trail of Tears, almost all the Cherokees who lived in Tennessee had been Christians for two generations.

Today, some Native Americans are studying their traditional religious beliefs, and many feel they can combine their Christian faith with a respect for their ancestral ways. That can be difficult. Allison Shaw was shocked by the stereotypes that some people held about Indians. One day, outside a movie theater where she had taken her two small children to see Disney's *Pocahontas*, another theater-goer said to her, "Everyone knows that Indians are devil worshipers." Allison corrected the woman but felt stung that

MELUNGEONS

An early English explorer named Abraham Wood mentions in his 1673 journal that he found living on the Tennessee River "a white people which have long beardes and whiskers and weares clothing." The settlers said that these people, who called themselves Melungeons, spoke English and practiced Christianity. They were light-skinned and tall, with black hair and eyes.

Melungeons still live in east Tennessee, mostly in very isolated Hancock County. There are several theories about their origin. Some believe they are the descendants of the first English settlers at Roanoke, who mysteriously disappeared in the sixteenth century. Others say they could be descendants of white explorers and escaped slaves who married Indians.

The Melungeons themselves say they are descended from Portuguese explorers. Since Melungeons suffer from diseases common to people from Mediterranean countries such as Portugal, their claim is likely to be true.

Many Cherokees keep their rich heritage alive, often using modern products, like these beads, in their traditional crafts.

a fellow Christian would have so little regard and understanding for someone else's beliefs.

Because of the large numbers of fundamentalist religions in the South, the area is sometimes called the Bible Belt. As the home of the sixteen-million-member Southern Baptist Convention, the largest group of Protestants in the United States, Tennessee is like the buckle on that belt. There are by far more Southern Baptists in Tennessee than followers of any other religion. Next come the

Sequatchie Valley

Methodists, followed by Presbyterians and members of the Church of Christ.

One unusual form of Protestantism exists mostly in the Appalachian Mountains of Tennessee and Kentucky: snake handling. A passage in the Bible (Mark 16:18) says, "They shall take up serpents and if they drink any deadly thing, it shall in no way hurt them." Snake handlers believe that this means that anyone who truly believes in Jesus and lives a good life can pick up poisonous snakes and drink poison and never be harmed.

To prove the depth of their faith, some believers may handle

Traditional Chinese dancers perform at Nashville's Summer Lights festival.

snakes and drink small amounts of poison in their religious services. Worshipers are occasionally bitten, sometimes fatally. Snake handling was made illegal in 1973 because of worries that children were being harmed. Still, in parts of Tennessee, Kentucky, and Indiana, a few churches still practice it.

While the majority of Tennesseans are Protestants, the Catholic and Jewish populations are growing, especially in the larger cities. Many Asians in middle Tennessee are bringing religions such as Buddhism to the area as well. When Eva Baker was a child in Nashville in the 1920s, everyone she knew was a Protestant. "It wasn't till I was in high school that I met my first Catholic," she says, "and it was a real shock to me!" Her son knew both Protestants and Catholics as a child, but did not have a Jewish acquaintance until he was in high school in the 1960s. In Nashville in the 1990s, his children have had Protestant, Catholic, Jewish, Buddhist, Hindu, Unitarian, Quaker, and atheist friends all their lives.

RACE RELATIONS

Nowhere is the division among the regions of Tennessee more obvious than in the history of race relations. Before the Civil War, slavery was more prevalent in the middle and western parts of the state than in the east, mostly because of the differences in ways of farming.

Carol Hamlett's ancestor Asa Robertson owned twenty-three slaves in west Tennessee in the 1850s. When her great-grand-parents gave some land to Crockett County in the 1940s for the purpose of building a school, they made it clear that the school was

FRIED CORN

Almost all the people who formed early communities in Tennessee counted on the fertile land to provide them with food. The inexperienced settlers of Rugby were so confident that they could earn money selling their surplus produce that they printed up labels for the cans they were going to use. One of them shows a large lady in long skirts on top of a ladder, cheerfully plucking tomatoes off a tree! Perhaps the reason the labels were never used is that the Rugbians discovered that tomatoes actually grow on a vine low to the ground.

The best recipes from Tennessee rely on what thrives here, especially fresh produce and hogs.

Have an adult help you cut the kernels off five ears of very fresh corn, preferably white. With a spoon, scrape the cobs to get out the small bits of corn that remain.

Melt two tablespoons of bacon grease in a large skillet. Add the corn, ½ teaspoon salt, a pinch of pepper, a pinch of sugar, and ¼ cup water. Cook over low heat, stirring occasionally, until corn is tender (about 10 minutes). Add a little more water if the corn starts to stick. Serve hot with ham and biscuits.

to be for white children only. Carol says, "When my mother moved down there from New York State in 1945, she was shocked to see that there were still slave cabins on the property."

Blacks, most of them slaves, were taken to Tennessee with the earliest settlers. Until the Civil War, both enslaved and free blacks in the state worked mostly on farms, with a smaller number in iron foundries or as house servants. When freedom came, few had the education or experience necessary to work in highly skilled jobs. It was a difficult fight to achieve some measure of equality.

Integration was slow, and conflicts were frequent. A major race riot erupted in the middle-Tennessee town of Columbia in 1946,

Bales of cotton are loaded at a mill.

following a fistfight between a black man and a white man. After four days of violence, two black men were dead, dozens had been beaten, and Columbia's entire black district was destroyed.

Even so, little by little, Tennesseans of different races began living together in relative harmony. The small towns of east Tennessee had included both black and white congregation members in most of their churches. During the nineteenth century, a time when blacks and whites were not even buried in the same graveyard, people of both races were interred at the City Cemetery of Nashville, making it, as far as anyone knows, the oldest integrated cemetery in the country.

Race relations are far from perfect in Tennessee. Yet Stacy Franklin, who moved to Nashville in 1989, feels far more at ease living here than she did in the North. Stacy, who is black, and Jack, her white husband, were frightened by racist taunting in the northern city where they both grew up. Stacy's sister moved to Nashville, and she advised Stacy, "Move down here—no one cares about mixed-race couples in Nashville." Stacy and Jack did just that and are happily raising their children in Nashville. "I feel more comfortable here than anyplace else," says Stacy.

Jill Martin disagrees. Jill, who is white, stopped attending her church after one of the congregation told her that her daughter's birth defect was God's punishment for Jill's marrying a black man. "I know she's not the only one who thinks that way," says Jill, still furious over the incident, which took place ten years ago. "I know I should forgive her, but God hasn't softened my heart that much yet."

Relations between Native Americans and people of European

ancestry in Tennessee have often been stormy. According to Allison Shaw, they are improving: "There's less prejudice here than in states where Indians live on reservations. Tennessee has always been a state that prides itself on valuing families and communities, and these have always been important to Indian people, too. There's very little discrimination in jobs and housing against Native peoples." She adds that the solidarity in the Native American community gives all of them strength: "Being Indian is like being part of this huge tapestry that has lots of colors and patterns and textures, but it's all woven from a single thread, and that thread runs through all of us. There are differences in culture, in language, in spiritual belief, but we are all tied together."

Native American women in traditional dress

5 DYNAMIC TENNESSEANS

Grand Ole Opry, Nashville

Mention Tennessee, especially Nashville, and most Americans think of country music. Tennesseans are indeed proud of their country stars, but the citizens of the Volunteer State have made important contributions in politics, civil rights, sports, and other areas as well.

PIONEERS AND POLITICIANS

Sadly, the names and achievements of most prominent Indians before the eighteenth century have been lost. One early leader was Nancy Ward, who was born in 1738. Her Cherokee name was Nanye'-hi, meaning Spirit People, and she was given the nickname Isistu-na-gis-ka, or Cherokee Rose.

Women were the traditional leaders of the Cherokees; it was only after the arrival of white settlers that men took over. The head of the women, known as Ghighau (the Honored Woman or War Woman), was part political leader, part priestess. As a seventeen-year-old mother of two, Nanye'-hi took her husband's place in battle after he was killed. She fought so bravely that the enemy was defeated and she was declared the Honored Woman.

Nanye'-hi was determined to befriend Tennessee's white settlers. She declared, "Our cry is for peace; let it continue. . . . This peace must last forever." She often relayed warnings of Cherokee attacks to the settlers. Nanye'-hi married a white settler named Bryan Ward and changed her first name to Nancy. Her great-grandson said that when she died in 1824, a light "rose from her body, fluttered like a bird around the room, and finally flew out the door."

David (Davy) Crockett was a scout under Andrew Jackson in the Creek Indian War, and he served as U.S. congressman from Tennessee. He strongly disagreed with Jackson about the Trail of Tears and was defeated for reelection in 1834. Bitterly, he told Tennessee's voters, "You can go to Hell; I'm going to Texas." He was one of only six survivors of the Battle of the Alamo in the fight for Texas's independence from Mexico, but after the battle he was shot by order of the Mexican general.

Sam Houston lived with the Cherokees after running away from

After resigning as governor of Tennessee, Sam Houston was formally adopted into the Cherokee nation.

home when he was fifteen. The Cherokees named him Raven for his black hair. He was first a schoolteacher in Maryville (near Knoxville), then a U.S. congressman. He was elected governor of Tennessee in 1827. He did not serve out his term but mysteriously resigned after his wife left him.

Houston returned to live with the Cherokees and then went to Texas, where he served in the Mexican War. He was governor of Texas, commander in chief of the Texas army, and first president of the Lone Star Republic. He led the troops that freed Texas from Mexico in 1836 and became a U.S. senator.

Sam Davis is known as the Boy Hero of the Confederacy. In 1863 he was captured while carrying papers showing information that had come from a Union soldier. He refused to tell who had given him the papers, even though he knew he would be executed as a spy. The day before his execution, he wrote a letter to his parents, saying, "Mother, tell the children to be good. I wish I could see you all once more, but I never will any more. Mother and father, do not forget me. Think of me when I am dead, but do not grieve for me; it will do no good." Just before he was hanged, the general told him he would be set free if he told who had given him the papers, but he said, "I would rather die a thousand deaths than betray a friend or be false to duty."

Ida B. Wells became a civil rights activist after three friends of hers were lynched. Earlier, some white people had wanted to sit in the no-smoking car of a train she was riding. Wells was told to move to a smoking car, and she refused to move. When the conductor tried to pull her out of her seat, she bit him and braced her feet against the seat ahead of her. It took several men to move her. She later sued the railroad. Although she lost the suit, her actions helped many people to see the injustice of segregation.

As a newspaper publisher in Memphis and Chicago, Wells led crusades against lynching. The offices housing her Memphis newspaper were destroyed in 1892 by whites who were angry at her outspoken views.

Albert Gore Jr., the son of a U.S. senator from Tennessee, was

Al Gore Jr. celebrates his father's 1958 reelection to the United States Senate, and his own vice-presidential nomination at the 1992 Democratic National Convention.

born in 1948, and became a United States senator and congressman. He was elected vice president of the United States under President Bill Clinton in 1992 and 1996. Gore, the author of a book on the environment, claims ecology as his main field of interest.

COUNTRY, BLUES, AND ROCK 'N' ROLL

Of course, country music is king in Tennessee, especially in Nashville. *Hee Haw*, videotaped in Nashville, is the longest-running syndicated show in the history of television. The Grand Ole Opry, which began radio broadcasts of country music in 1925, is in Nashville too. Other kinds of music are important in the state as well. The blues was born in Memphis, and bluegrass music sprang up in the middle and eastern parts of the state and in Kentucky.

Nashville's nickname, Music City, was inspired by the Fisk Jubilee Singers. Just a few years after its founding as a university for black students, Fisk University was in desperate shape: The buildings were falling apart, food supplies were low, teachers were underpaid, and the school had huge debts. Using borrowed money, Fisk's music professor took his Fisk Jubilee Singers on a tour of the United States and Europe. President Ulysses S. Grant invited them to sing in the White House. The singers triumphantly returned home with enough funds to buy more land and help build Jubilee Hall at Fisk.

Composer W. C. Handy, known as the Father of the Blues, lived in the early 1900s on Beale Street in Memphis. He is credited with inventing the blues, a mixture of jazz and traditional work songs. "Memphis Blues" and "Beale Street Blues" are among his best-

W. C. Handy is credited with bringing the blues to an international audience.

known compositions. One of the most famous blues singers, Bessie Smith, was born in Chattanooga. She sang for pennies on the streets of her hometown before being discovered.

Aretha Franklin, "First Lady of Soul," and rock legend Tina Turner are Tennesseans. So was popular singer Dinah Shore. Pat Boone, who has sold more than fifty million records, had his own television show, and starred in fifteen movies, is originally from Nashville.

Elvis Presley taught himself to play guitar. He was born in Tupelo, Mississippi, and as a boy he sang in church and at revival meetings in Mississippi and later in Memphis, Tennessee. Presley was discovered in Memphis while he was working as a truck driver. His new brand of music, merging rock and roll with the

Aretha Franklin, "First Lady of Soul," at the 1993 Essence Awards. She started out as a gospel singer and made her first recording when she was twelve years old.

Dolly Parton's exuberance is one of the traits her fans love most about her.

rhythm-and-blues style of his adopted hometown, became wildly popular. Presley died, possibly of a drug overdose, in his Memphis home in 1977.

Dolly Parton was born into a large family in Locust Ridge, near Sevierville in east Tennessee. Although the family was poor, they were very close, and Dolly's parents encouraged their daughter's love of music. She first came to the public's attention as a member of Porter Wagoner's band in 1967. In 1974, Parton left Wagoner and toured the world with her own band. She has won three Grammy Awards, American music's highest honor. In 1980, Parton launched a successful career as an actress, with the film *9 to 5*. Other films quickly followed, but she has never given up her singing career, continuing to win music awards through the 1990s.

LITERATURE

Sequoyah, half Cherokee and half white, was born in east Tennessee around 1760. He developed an alphabet for the Cherokees. Since the Cherokee language contained sounds not represented by English letters, he invented new ones for his written language, which took him twelve years to develop. The language was easier to learn than written English, and in a few years the Cherokees of east Tennessee were more literate than the white population that lived near them.

The Native American newspaper the *Cherokee Phoenix* has been published since 1827. The sequoia redwoods of the West Coast are named in honor of this great man.

Knoxville native James Agee's novel *A Death in the Family* won

A DEATH IN THE FAMILY

Agee's recollections of Knoxville "in the time that I lived there so successfully disguised to myself as a child" inspired this description of a summer evening:

On the rough wet grass of the back yard my father and mother have spread quilts. We all lie there, my mother, my father, my uncle, my aunt, and I too am lying there. First we were sitting up, then one of us lay down, and then we all lay down, on our stomachs, or on our sides, or on our backs, and they have kept on talking. They are not talking much, and the talk is quiet, of nothing in particular, of nothing at all in particular, of nothing at all. The stars are wide and alive, they seem each like a smile of great sweetness, and they seem very near. All my people are larger bodies than mine, quiet, with voices gentle and meaningless like the voices of sleeping birds. One is an artist, he is living at home. One is a musician, she is living at home. One is my mother who is good to me. One is my father who is good to me. By some chance, here they are, all on this earth; and who shall ever tell the sorrow of being on this earth, lying, on quilts, on the grass, in a summer evening, among the sounds of night. May God bless my people, my uncle, my aunt, my mother, my good father, oh, remember them kindly in their time of trouble; and in the hour of their taking away.

After a little I am taken in and put to bed. Sleep, soft smiling, draws me unto her: and those receive me, who quietly treat me, as one familiar and well-beloved in that home: but will not, not now, not ever; but will not ever tell me who I am.

the Pulitzer Prize in 1958. The play based on this book, *All the Way Home*, was also awarded a Pulitzer just three years later. Agee's powerful study of the lives of poor southern farmers during the Depression, *Let Us Now Praise Famous Men*, drew the country's awareness to their plight and shocked many readers. He also worked as a Hollywood scriptwriter. His best-known film is *The African Queen*, which starred Humphrey Bogart and Katharine Hepburn.

Alex Haley was born in Ithaca, New York, in 1921, but grew up in Henning, near Memphis. His first book, *The Autobiography of Malcolm X* (written with civil rights leader Malcolm X), was an

Alex Haley's Roots *sparked an interest in genealogy.*

instant success. But his fame rests with his second book, *Roots: The Saga of an American Family*, a fictionalized account of his ancestors from their time in Africa, through slavery, to the modern day. *Roots* was one of the biggest best-sellers of all time and won a special Pulitzer Prize in 1977. It was made into one of the first and most watched televised miniseries, which was nominated for thirty-seven Emmy awards.

The author Ishmael Reed was born in Chattanooga in 1938. Although he grew up in Buffalo, New York, Tennessee is a frequent subject of his writings. One of his collections of poems is entitled *Chattanooga*. In 1973, two of his books were nominated for the National Book Award, one a volume of poetry, the other fiction. Reed has always been an outspoken critic of the condition of black Americans and continues today to voice strong opinions about race relations in the United States.

THE ARTS

"This here is miracles I can do. Can't nobody do these but me. I can't help carving. I just does it." The speaker is William Edmondson, who was born around 1883 in Nashville, where his parents had been slaves. Edmondson worked at various jobs until he retired in his fifties. One day he heard a voice that he said belonged to God, whom he called his "heavenly daddy." The voice said, "Will, cut that stone . . . and it better be limestone too."

Edmondson used blocks of limestone left over from building projects and began carving tombstones with homemade chisels and files. He gave away many of them, saying that he made them not for profit but because God had ordered him to. Soon he was carving birds, strange animals he called "critters," angels, figures from the Bible, preachers, and other subjects.

After about five years, his work was noticed, but as he said, "I didn't know I was no artist till them folks come and told me I was." His sculptures were exhibited in the first one-man show by a black artist in the history of New York's Museum of Modern Art. William Edmondson died in 1951.

Red Grooms was born in Nashville in 1937. He attended George Peabody College for Teachers in Nashville, as well as art school. He is well known for his delightful sculptures, some of which are large enough to walk around in. Many of his constructions depict various aspects of modern life, such as a subway train or people

Mr. and Mrs. Rembrandt, *by Red Grooms*

standing on an escalator, but there is always something odd about the setting or the people. The escalator riders, for example, while holding a briefcase and reading a newspaper, might be completely naked. The people on the subway might have distorted faces. Grooms's works are in the permanent collections of many museums, including the Cheekwood Fine Arts Center in Nashville, the Chicago Art Institute, Washington D.C.'s Hirshhorn Museum and Sculpture Garden, and the Museum of Modern Art.

STAGE AND SCREEN

Patricia Neal, born in Knoxville in 1926, is a stage and screen actress. She won an Oscar for the film *Hud*, which also starred Paul Newman. After recovering from three major strokes, she said, "The neurosurgeon thought I would conk out, but Tennessee hillbillies don't conk out that easy."

Oprah Winfrey, "Queen of Daytime TV," is the daughter of Vernon Winfrey, a former Nashville Metro City Council member. She left Tennessee as a teenager, returning to attend Tennessee State University. While Winfrey was a student, she became the first Miss Black Tennessee at age eighteen. She started her broadcast career at Nashville's Channel 5. From there she moved on to other cities and eventually to the career that has made her famous.

SPORTS

Tennessee has no major-league sports teams to date, although in 1996 the Houston Oilers announced their intention to move to

Nashville. Still, a lot goes on here in the sports world. The University of Tennessee's Neyland Stadium in Knoxville is larger than many professional teams' stadiums, seating almost one hundred thousand spectators. Memphis is the site of the Liberty Bowl, an important college football event.

Baseball is popular in Tennessee, with minor-league teams in Memphis, Knoxville, Chattanooga, and Nashville, which has a AAA team.

Auto racing is a popular sport throughout the state, which hosts several NASCAR races. The Nashville Motor Speedway runs races from May through October, and the Southeastern 500 is held in Bristol.

Memphis hosts the National Indoor Tennis Tournament and the Danny Thomas Memphis Golf Classic.

Some important figures in the sports world have called Tennessee home. Satchel (Leroy Robert) Paige was a star pitcher in the Negro leagues, baseball teams for black players at a time when sports were segregated. He played for both the Nashville Elite Giants and the Chattanooga Black Lookouts. Paige pitched in about twenty-five hundred games, winning about two thousand of them and pitching an incredible fifty no-hitters. After major-league baseball was integrated in 1947, Paige joined the Cleveland Indians at the age of forty-two. He won six games and lost only one.

The first former star of the Negro leagues to be elected to the Baseball Hall of Fame, Paige may well have been the greatest pitcher of all time. He was well known for his wit and humor as well as his pitching. His personal slogan was "Don't look back—something may be gaining on you." He died in 1982.

In 1934, Satchel Paige pitched 105 games and won 104 of them.

Tennessee State University's women's track team, the Tigerbelles, has produced forty Olympians. In the 1956 Summer Olympics in Austria, only six medals were won by American women—five of them by Tigerbelles. The most famous Tigerbelle, Wilma Rudolph, was born in 1940, the twentieth of twenty-two children, in Bethlehem, Tennessee, and raised in Clarksville. She was a sickly girl who lost the use of one leg after contracting polio at age four. Her family refused to believe the doctors who said she would never walk again. They took her to Nashville for treatments, massaged her leg, and helped her exercise. Wilma justified their faith in her when she walked at age eight. After starring with the Tigerbelles, Rudolph set two world records in the 1960 Olympics, winning three gold medals.

After she retired from sports, Wilma Rudolph became a spokesperson for civil rights. She was named an official goodwill ambassador to western Africa. In 1996, the people of her home-town of Clarksville erected a statue to her on the newly renamed Wilma Rudolph Boulevard.

PIGGLY WIGGLY

It's hard for a modern person to imagine going shopping before the days of Clarence Saunders of Memphis. Before his time, there were no self-service stores. A customer had to give an order to a clerk and wait for the clerk to locate everything that was requested. Customers often had to wait a long time for a clerk to be free, and all this service made groceries more expensive. Saunders invented the supermarket in response. Inspired, he later said, by seeing the struggles of a pig trying to get under a fence, he called his store Piggly Wiggly.

Clarence Saunders's home in Memphis is called the Pink Palace. It houses a museum and traveling exhibits.

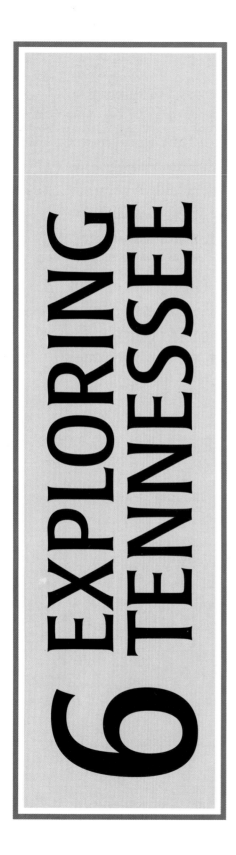

6 EXPLORING TENNESSEE

6 WILSON BARN

Tennessee is very popular with vacationers. Great Smoky Mountains National Park, in east Tennessee and North Carolina, is the most popular of all national parks in the United States, hosting some eighty million visitors every year. More tour buses go to Nashville than to any other city in the country; millions of people visit Graceland, Elvis Presley's Memphis home; and in between, visitors can find spectacular scenery, charming small towns, and lively festivals.

Tennessee's beautiful scenery draws sportspeople as well. The world's largest artificial ski surface is in Gatlinburg, in the Smokies. People travel from all over the world to explore Tennessee's caves and mountains. So exciting are the white-water rapids that the 1996 Summer Olympics, held in Atlanta, moved to Tennessee's Ocoee River for the white-water events.

THE MOUNTAINOUS EAST

Great Smoky Mountains National Park is the major attraction of east Tennessee. The Cherokees called the area the Land of a Thousand Smokes because of the haze that hangs over the mountains. Today, the 500,000-acre park is home to many birds, mammals, and plants. You can find twenty-six species of salamander—more than in any other area of the same size.

The beautiful Smokies beckon hikers and picnickers.

Gatlinburg is the town nearest the park. Its population of thirty-six thousand is overwhelmed by the more than four million visitors who pass through each year. Crammed with motels and souvenir shops, Gatlinburg exists for the tourist trade.

About five miles away is Pigeon Forge, where Dolly Parton's theme park, Dollywood, houses crafts shops and other attractions. The big draw, though, is country music.

Knoxville is the largest city in the eastern portion of the state. It has come a long way since author John Gunther wrote in 1946,

Lee Ogle makes brooms by hand in this Gatlinburg workshop.

"Knoxville is the ugliest city I ever saw in America [and] is one of the least orderly cities in the South." Home to the largest campus of the University of Tennessee, Knoxville hosted the 1982 World's Fair. The three-hundred-foot-tall tower of the Sunsphere still stands at the site of the fair.

The Knoxville Museum of Art, housed near the Eleventh Avenue Artists' Colony of art galleries and studios, offers music and lectures as well as art works. Every April, the city's Dogwood Festival attracts visitors who can walk six different dogwood trails and attend many different crafts fairs and concerts.

Also in east Tennessee is Oak Ridge, where the developers of the atom bomb worked in secrecy. The American Museum of Science and Energy, developed by the United States Department of Energy, is one of the world's largest museums devoted to this topic.

Jonesborough hosts the National Storytelling Festival in October. This festival grows each year, as storytellers from all over the United States and around the world come to learn more about their art, to hear other tellers' stories, and to enter competitions.

PLATEAU AND VALLEY REGION

Chattanooga is home to Lookout Mountain. The Cherokee name for this towering cliff was Chatunuga, which means "the rock which comes to an end." Here you will find the Incline Railway, the world's steepest passenger railroad. The mountain is so tall that on a good day a visitor can see seven states from its peak. An important Civil War conflict, called the Battle Above the Clouds, was fought on Lookout Mountain in 1863, and nearby is the largest

A cannon from the Civil War sits on top of Lookout Mountain above Chattanooga.

and oldest military park in the United States: Chickamauga and Chattanooga National Military Park.

The natural wonders outside Chattanooga also attract many visitors. Nearby is Ruby Falls, which at 260 feet is the highest underground waterfall in America. The falls is 1,120 feet below

PLACES TO SEE

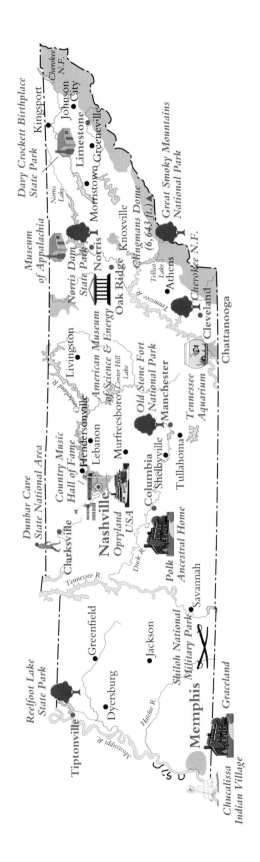

Reelfoot Lake
State Park

Tiptonville

Greenfield

Dyersburg

Jackson

Mississippi R.

Hatchie R.

Memphis

Graceland

Shiloh National
Military Park

Savannah

Chucalissa
Indian Village

Tennessee R.

Clarksville

Dunbar Cave
State National Area

Nashville

Opryland
USA

Country Music
Hall of Fame

Hendersonville

Lebanon

Livingston

Cumberland R.

Murfreesboro

Columbia

Polk
Ancestral Home

Duck R.

Shelbyville

Tullahoma

Manchester

Old Stone Fort
National Park

American Museum
of Science & Energy

Center Hill
Lake

Tennessee
Aquarium

Chattanooga

Museum
of Appalachia

Norris Dam
State Park

Norris

Norris
Lake

Oak Ridge

Knoxville

Clingmans Dome
(6,643 ft.)

Great Smoky Mountains
National Park

Tennessee R.

Tellico
Lake

Athens

Cleveland

Cherokee N.F.

Davy Crockett Birthplace
State Park

Kingsport

Johnson
City

Limestone

Morristown Greeneville

Cherokee
N.F.

Cherokee

the ground. Rock City, a park with caves, rock formations, and oddly shaped boulders, is a popular spot for tourists.

Chattanooga is home to the Tennessee Aquarium, which opened in 1992. This is the first large freshwater-fish aquarium in the world. Visitors take an elevator to the top of the museum, then walk down the spiraling ramp, following the course of a stream from the Smoky Mountains to the Gulf of Mexico. Along the way, natural habitats are recreated, with three hundred fifty species of mammals, birds, reptiles, and fish.

Cumberland Mountain State Rustic Park, near Crossville, was built during the Great Depression by members of the Civilian Conservation Corps, local men who learned construction work while providing cabins and clearings for others to enjoy. The cabins in the park are built mainly of the local Crab Orchard stone, a honey-colored rock that abounds in the hills. The park also has campgrounds, a lake, and nature trails. Nearby is Fall Creek Falls State Park, which boasts a 256-foot waterfall, the highest east of the Rockies.

MIDDLE TENNESSEE

Nashville may be the state capital, but it is the country music that draws crowds of visitors each year. Not all Nashvilleans love this popular American music, however. Greg Giles says, "Nashville used to be known as the 'Athens of the South' because of all the universities here. It was recognized for being a center of culture and learning."

Middle Tennessee is an area rich in history. Nashville has been

Despite its nickname of Music City, U.S.A., Nashville is a thriving commercial city where music takes a backseat to insurance and health-care industries.

the capital since 1826. The capitol building was completed in 1859, making it one of the oldest state capitols in the country.

When Tennessee celebrated its one hundredth birthday in 1896, Nashville was still known as the Athens of the South. One of the most popular exhibits in the Centennial Exposition was a full-sized wood-and-plaster copy of the Parthenon, the most famous monument of ancient Athens. When the original building disintegrated, it was rebuilt in concrete in Centennial Park, and today it is the symbol of the city.

Nashville and its surrounding area have many attractions for anyone interested in history. The State Museum in downtown Nashville has exhibits on the history of the state, beginning with prehistoric times. Fort Nashborough on the banks of the Cumberland River is a replica of the original fort built by the settlers.

In Smyrna, outside Nashville, a visitor can tour the home of the Boy Hero of the Confederacy. Tour guides dressed in nineteenth-century costume lead visitors through the house and grounds, telling Sam Davis's story and showing what life on a prosperous farm of the time was like. Every May, the grounds come alive for Sam Davis Days, as blacksmiths, weavers, soap makers, candle dippers, whittlers, and other craftspeople demonstrate the kinds of work that the Davis family and their slaves would have done every day.

The Hermitage, Andrew Jackson's home, is also open to the public. Like Sam Davis's home, Jackson's gracious white house is furnished with nineteenth-century furniture.

Still, the big draw for most tourists in middle Tennessee is country music. Nashville's six-block Music Row includes many souvenir shops as well as the Country Music Hall of Fame and the Country Music Wax Museum. The historic Ryman Auditorium, originally constructed as a religious revival house, was the original home of the Grand Ole Opry. Major reconstruction in 1995 restored the building to its original appearance. The Opry now broadcasts from Opryland, U.S.A., on the eastern border of the city.

The Parthenon houses the world's largest indoor sculpture, a forty-two foot statue of the goddess Athena.

"IF IT AIN'T COUNTRY, IT AIN'T MUSIC"

There are more country-music radio stations in America than any other kind. This popular form of American music has its roots in the folk music of England, Ireland, and Scotland. It was brought to America from the seventeenth through the nineteenth centuries and adapted by the people living in the southeast.

As interest in this music grew, George D. Hay, a Memphis-born radio announcer, started a new show called *National Barn Dance* on a Chicago radio station in the 1920s. He moved the show to Nashville in 1925 and began broadcasting *Barn Dance* on radio station WSM.

Although the name of the program was soon changed to *The Grand Ole Opry*, the stage set still features a farm setting with a large barn in the middle. In 1943, the Opry moved to Nashville's thirty-three-hundred-seat Ryman Auditorium in Nashville. The program was first televised seven years later. By 1974 the Opry had outgrown the Ryman Auditorium, and it moved to the Opryland Theme Park in east Nashville. The Opry theater is now the world's largest broadcast studio.

The 120-acre amusement park, Opryland Theme Park, is also located there, as is the Opryland Hotel, a major convention center.

Nashville is also home to two museums for children. The Nashville Toy Museum has exhibits of toys from centuries ago through the present. The Cumberland Science Museum hosts traveling scientific shows and has a planetarium as well as many permanent exhibits. Most of these are interactive, allowing the visitor to find out firsthand the scientific principles involved.

Most of Nashville's festivals celebrate music. City Lights, held downtown every June, attracts bands of every kind to its large outdoor stages. Fan Fair, also in June, gives fans a chance to meet their favorite stars. This popular event celebrated its tenth anniversary in 1996 by selling out all twenty-four thousand tickets before the show even began.

Country isn't the only kind of music performed in Nashville!

The Tennessee walking horse, famous for its unusually fast and smooth walk, comes from middle Tennessee. Every year, the town of Shelbyville hosts the Tennessee Walking Horse Celebration, where these animals are shown and judged. Horses are also bought and sold at the celebration, along with all sorts of riding gear and souvenirs. In 1994, more than two thousand horses were registered at the event, which awarded $600,000 in prizes.

Farther south, near Manchester, is the mysterious Old Stone Fort. This huge structure, which includes a moat, was built by Indians before the arrival of the settlers, but when and for what purpose is now unknown.

Carbon Copy, world champion Tennessee walking horse

THE FLATLANDS

The major attraction of west Tennessee is Memphis, with Elvis Presley's home, Graceland. Preserved as a shrine to the "King," as Presley is known, Graceland is the second-most-visited home in America (after the White House). People come to see where Presley lived with his wife and daughter and to admire the many sequined costumes worn by the performer. His tomb is often covered with flowers left by fans.

Memphis is more than Graceland, though. Music lovers flock to Beale Street, where the purely American form of music known as the blues was born. Concerts and performances, indoors and out-doors, showcase both traditional and modern forms of the blues.

The reconstructed Chucalissa Indian Village shows what life in an Indian town was like before the coming of the settlers. It is located on the site of an Indian town that existed for about seven centuries. Archaeologists have been excavating there, and several houses and a temple have been rebuilt.

Mud Island, in the middle of the Mississippi River, is home to several attractions, including an amphitheater and a theme park. The River Walk is a small-scale reproduction of the entire course of the Mississippi. The Mississippi River Museum has exhibits on the history and ecology of the longest river in North America.

Memphis, Egypt, is located on the longest river in the continent of Africa, so Memphis, Tennessee, was named for the ancient Egyptian city. To celebrate the "sisterhood" of the two cities, the Tennessee city built a thirty-two-story, stainless-steel pyramid on the banks of the Mississippi River. The pyramid opened to the public in 1991.

Admirers leave letters and gifts for Elvis Presley at the foot of this statue in Memphis.

Elvis Presley's home, Graceland

The Lorraine Motel, where Martin Luther King Jr. was assassinated, has been turned into the National Civil Rights Museum. The struggle of African Americans to achieve equal rights is chronicled here, with special attention to King's Nobel Peace Prize-winning work.

One of the most popular attractions in Memphis is the twice-daily duck parade at the Peabody Hotel. Every morning a line of ducks waddles out to the lobby. Then they walk solemnly up velvet-covered steps to the fountain, where they swim all day. The performance is repeated in reverse in the evening when they strut down the steps and back to the elevator, then to the pen in their luxury penthouse to spend the night.

Memphis hosts a month-long festival called Memphis in May that celebrates a different country each year. Food, music, art, and performances from that country turn the city into a big party every evening and weekend in May.

In upper west Tennessee is thirteen-thousand-acre Reelfoot Lake. Its tranquil beauty and rich wildlife attract not only people who are interested in fishing, but also naturalists, who find a high concentration of bald eagles and other birds here. Eagle Watch Tours start in January and continue through March, the months when these magnificent birds fly through on their migratory route. "When I went to Reelfoot to see the bald eagles," remembers Sam Turner, "I thought, Big deal, they're just a big bird. But then when one swooped down, caught a fish, and then perched on a branch eating it, glaring at the people with one big eye, I realized it was truly awesome. We all stopped talking and looked at it as long as it sat on its branch. What a majestic creature!"

Majestic creatures, a romantic history, lofty mountains, fertile plains, friendly people—no wonder Tennesseans are proud of their state. People lucky enough to call Tennessee home are reluctant to move away, and newcomers quickly feel welcome and put down their own roots. Explore Tennessee and see its majesty for yourself!

The Appalachian Trail in the Tennessee Smokies. This trail now runs the entire length of the range, offering hikers an easy entry into a wilderness that blocked early settlers from moving west.

THE FLAG: The state flag of Tennessee has three white stars in a blue circle with a white ring around it. The three stars stand for the three parts of Tennessee--east, middle, and west. A thin white line at the right side of the flag separates the red background from a blue band. The flag was adopted in 1905.

THE SEAL: On the state seal, a plow, wheat, and a cotton plant stand for agriculture in Tennessee. A riverboat represents commerce, or trade, in the state. The date 1796 is the year Tennessee became a state and approved its first constitution. The Roman number for 16 (XVI), at the top of the seal, shows that Tennessee is the sixteenth state. The seal was first used during the term of Governor William G. Brownlow, who served from 1865 to 1869.

STATE SURVEY

Statehood: June 1, 1796

Origin of Name: Name comes from "Tanasie," a Cherokee village in the area.

Nickname: Volunteer State or Big Bend State

Capital: Nashville

Motto: Agriculture and Commerce

Bird: Mockingbird

Flower: Iris

Tree: Tulip poplar

Mineral: Limestone

Gem: Freshwater pearl

Mockingbird

Iris

GEOGRAPHY

Highest Point: 6,643 feet above sea level, at Clingman's Dome

Lowest Point: 182 feet above sea level, in Shelby County

Area: 42,144 square miles

WHEN IT'S IRIS TIME IN TENNESSEE

Tennessee has six official state songs! This graceful waltz, honoring the official state flower, was adopted by the state legislature in 1935. Included among the other state songs are "The Tennessee Waltz" and "Rocky Top."

By Willa Mae Wald

Greatest Distance, North to South: 116 miles

Greatest Distance, East to West: 482 miles

Largest Cave: Cumberland Caverns

Bordering States: Kentucky and Virginia to the north; North Carolina to the east; Georgia, Alabama, and Mississippi to the south; and Arkansas and Missouri to the west

Hottest Recorded Temperature: 113°F at Perryville on July 29 and August 9, 1930

Coldest Recorded Temperature: –32°F at Mountain City on December 30, 1917

Average Annual Precipitation: 50 inches

Major Rivers: Big Sandy, Buffalo, Caney Fork, Clinch, Cumberland, Duck, Elk, Forked Deer, French Broad, Harpeth, Hatchee, Hiwassee, Holston, Little Tennessee, Loosahatchie, Mississippi, Obion, Powell, Sequatchie, Stones, Tennessee, Wolf

Major Lakes: Boone, Cherokee, Chickamauga, Douglas, Fort Loudoun, Fort Patrick Henry, Norris, Pickwick, Reelfoot, Watauga, Watts Bar

Mountains: Appalachian, Bald, Blue Ridge, Chilhowee, Cumberland, Great Smoky, Holston, Iron, Roan, Stone, Unicoi

Trees: ash, beech, cedar, cherry, cypress, elm, hickory, maple, red and white oaks, shortleaf pine, sycamore, walnut, yellow poplar

Wild Plants: azalea, dragonroot, hop clover, iris, mountain laurel, rhodo-dendron, spring-beauty, yellow jasmine

Animals: beaver, black bear, bobcat, fox, muskrat, possum, rabbit, raccoon, skunk, snake, white squirrel, white-tailed deer, wild hog

Game Birds: Canada goose, duck, quail, wild turkey

Birds: anhinga, bald eagle, egret, hawk, heron, marten, mockingbird, owl, raven, robin

Fish: bass, catfish, crappie, rainbow trout, wall-eyed pike

Endangered Animals: Alabama lamp mussel, Appalachian elktoe (mussel), Bachman's sparrow, barrens topminnow, Carolina northern flying squirrel, catspaw (mussel), Eastern cougar, lake sturgeon, national crayfish, pallid sturgeon, peregrine falcon, red wolf, red woodpecker, southern club shell (mussel), southern hickorynut mussel

Red wolf

Endangered Plants: American water-pennywort, American yew, Blue Ridge goldenrod, Carolina anemone, leafed trillium, leafy prairie-clover, Roan mountain bluet, Ruth's golden aster, purple fringeless orchid, skunk cabbage, sweet fern, Tennessee coneflower, white fringeless orchid, yellow fringeless orchid

TIMELINE

Tennessee History

c. 11,000 B.C. Paleo Indians come to Tennessee area during Ice Age

c. 6000 B.C. Archaic Indians chase Paleo Indians from area

c. 1000 B.C. Woodland Indians drive Archaic Indians from land

1540 Hernando de Soto of Spain becomes first European to explore Tennessee region

1673 English, Canadian, and French explorers come to Tennessee area

1772 East Tennessee settlers (the Watauga Association) write their own constitution

1775 Daniel Boone finds the Cumberland Gap in the mountains, opening the way for pioneers to go west

1775–1783 The American Revolution

1779 The first city in Tennessee, Jonesborough, is founded

1784 East Tennessee breaks away from North Carolina to form its own country, the Republic of Franklin

1789 The Territory of Tennessee is created

1796 Tennessee becomes the sixteenth state and approves its first constitution

1812 The War of 1812 breaks out between England and the United States

1829 Andrew Jackson of Tennessee becomes president of the United States

1834 The right to vote is taken away from free blacks

1838 The federal government forces the Cherokee out of Tennessee (Trail of Tears)

1843 Nashville becomes the state capital

1844 Tennessee governor James K. Polk is elected president

1861 The Civil War begins; Tennessee is the last state to secede from (leave) the Union

1862 The Battle of Shiloh is fought in Tennessee

1864 The Battle of Nashville, the last major conflict in the state, is fought

1865 The Civil War ends; Andrew Johnson of Tennessee becomes president after Lincoln's assassination

1866 Tennessee becomes the first state to return to the Union

1870 Tennessee draws up its third constitution and gives all male citizens 21 or older the right to vote

1878 Yellow fever kills 5,152 people in Memphis

1920 Tennessee becomes the thirty-sixth state to give women the right to vote

1933 Congress creates the Tennessee Valley Authority (TVA)

1942 The federal government begins building the atomic energy center at Oak Ridge

1956 Tennessee begins school integration

1964 The first African American is elected to the Tennessee legislature

1968 Martin Luther King Jr. is assassinated in Memphis

1982 Knoxville hosts the World's Fair

1996 Tennessee's first African-American chief justice is appointed to the state Supreme Court

ECONOMY

Agricultural Products: cattle, corn, cotton, dairy products, fruit, hogs, lumber, poultry, sheep, soybeans, tobacco, vegetables, wheat

Tobacco

Manufactured Products: chemicals, clothing, electrical and electronic equipment, food processing, food products, machinery, metal products, paper products, plastic products, printed materials, rubber products, transportation equipment

Natural Resources: ball clay, barite, coal, copper, crushed stone, fluorite, gravel, iron, lignite, limestone, marble, natural gas, petroleum, phosphate rock, pyrite, sand, zinc

Business and Trade: agriculture, banking, construction, insurance, manufacturing (including automobiles), mining, real estate, service industry, transportation, wholesale and retail trade

CALENDAR OF CELEBRATIONS

Eagle Watch Tours Every January through March, visitors can get a close-up look at the many bald eagles that make their winter home in Reelfoot Lake.

Mule Day Festival During the first week of April, Columbia celebrates its fame as the mule-raising capital of Tennessee with a mule-pulling parade, mule shows, down-home cooking, and arts and crafts.

Dogwood Arts Festival A 17-day festival is held every April in Knoxville to celebrate the dogwood trees in bloom in the city.

World's Biggest Fish Fry April in Paris, Tennessee, is the time for eating the best-tasting catfish, served at the fairgrounds.

Memphis in May International Festival For the entire month of May, Memphis holds plays, concerts, fairs, and the Cotton Maker's Jubilee, the largest African-American parade.

Tennessee Crafts Fair Held the first week of May, Centennial Park in Nashville is alive with art displays, a puppet theater, crafts demonstrations, and children's craft activities.

Tennessee Strawberry Festival The first or second week of May is when the town of Dayton has a 10-day children's fair, with sports events, a quilt show, a carnival, storytelling, and the world's longest strawberry shortcake.

Summer Lights Held at the end of May or at the beginning of June, this music festival in Nashville has bands of every kind playing on large outdoor stages.

Rhododendron Festival The middle of June brings the rhododendron festival to Roan Mountain, along with mountain music, dancing, food, and wildlife tours.

Summer Lights

International Country Music Fan Fair Nashville in mid-June is when fans have a chance to meet their favorite country music stars.

Old-Time Fiddlers' Jamboree and Crafts Festival In early July, country music and crafts fill the streets of the Smithville Square, where the town holds a "fiddle-off" to pick the best fiddler.

Appalachian Fair For a week in mid-August, Gray, Tennessee, hosts a huge fair featuring a carnival, farm displays, tractor pulls, baking contests, entertainment, and crafts from Appalachia.

Elvis Week Mid-August in Memphis brings citywide celebrations, including a tour of Elvis's junior high school and his early recording studio.

Tennessee Walking Horse Celebration For 10 days at the end of August, Shelbyville celebrates the Tennessee walking horse, with a contest for choosing the National Grand Champion of the breed. A dog show and petting zoo add to the fun.

International Banana Festival September brings this four-day festival to South Fulton, with a banana-eating contest and a parade featuring a one-ton banana pudding.

Apple Festival Held in Erwin on the last weekend of September, this celebration features music and dancing, food, crafts, a pottery show and sale, and a 4-mile footrace.

Reelfoot Lake Arts and Crafts Festival Reelfoot Lake State Park hosts a large arts and crafts festival at the beginning of October.

Heritage Days Held the first weekend of October at the home of Sam Davis, the "Boy Hero of the Confederacy," this festival in Smyrna features blacksmiths, weavers, and others who show how the Davis family and their slaves lived during the Civil War.

National Storytelling Festival On the first weekend of October, the historic town of Jonesborough holds a three-day festival that brings the best storytellers and stories from around the world.

Autumn Gold Festival Early in October, Coker Creek celebrates two types of gold: the gold found in creeks and on the leaves of the trees in the fall. The fun includes panning for gold and dancing and singing to mountain music.

Mountain Makin's Festival Eastern Tennessee hosts one of Tennessee's finest crafts shows each October. Mountain music is also played to add to the fun.

Christmas in the Park The Christmas season is celebrated at Cove Lake State Recreational Park Area, where music, lights, and decorations brighten the holiday.

STATE STARS

Roy Acuff (1903–1992), born in Maynardville, Tennessee, earned the nickname King of Country Music. He is best known for his hit song "The Wabash Cannonball." With his band, the Smoky Mountain Boys, Acuff made Tennessee music popular around the world. He also ran unsuccessfully for governor of Tennessee in 1948.

Roy Acuff

James Agee (1909–1955), one of the great Southern writers, was born in Knoxville. His novel *A Death in the Family* won the first Pulitzer Prize given for a book and the play based on it. Agee also wrote Hollywood films. His most famous was *The African Queen*.

Lamar Alexander (1940–   ) was governor of Tennessee from 1978 to 1987. He also served as Secretary of Education under Ronald Reagan. In 1996, Alexander was a candidate for the Republican nomination for president.

Howard Baker (1925–   ), born in Huntsville, Tennessee, was both the Senate majority leader (1981–1985) and the Senate minority leader (1977–1981). Baker became famous for leading the investigation of the Watergate scandal during the administration of President Richard Nixon. He also served as Ronald Reagan's chief of staff.

Howard Baker

Julian Bond (1940–   ) of Nashville was one of the nation's foremost civil rights leaders in the 1960s. In 1968, Bond became the first African American to be nominated for vice president.

Daniel Boone (1734–1820) was one of the early pioneers to explore the frontier regions of Tennessee and Kentucky. In 1775, Boone found the Cumberland Gap in the mountains around Tennessee. His discovery paved the way for pioneers to make their way west across the Appalachians.

Dorothy Brown (1919–   ) was the first African-American woman in the

South to practice surgery. She was also the first black woman to serve in the Tennessee legislature.

David (Davy) Crockett (1786–1836) was not "born on a mountaintop in Tennessee," as the song says, but in a log cabin near Limestone Creek. During his lifetime, Crockett was a scout in the Creek War (1813–1814), a member of Congress from Tennessee, a writer, and a soldier. He lived through the Battle of the Alamo but was shot on orders of the enemy leader.

Sam Davis (1842–1863) of Smyrna, Tennessee, was called the Boy Hero of the Confederacy. He was hanged as a spy during the Civil War for passing secret information given to him by a Union soldier. Davis refused to reveal the name of the soldier. Before hanging, Davis told the Confederate soldiers who had captured him that he would rather die a thousand deaths than betray a friend.

David Farragut (1801–1870) of Stony Point, Tennessee, joined the U.S. Navy at age nine. At age twelve, he was in charge of a ship. A Civil War hero, Farragut helped the Union win the war. In 1866, he became the first U.S. admiral of the navy.

David Farragut

Cornelia Fort (1919–1943) of Nashville was the first American woman pilot to die in service to her country. While she was flying a plane across Texas, a male pilot tried to scare her by flying too close. The planes collided, and both pilots were killed.

Aretha Franklin (1942–   ), born in Memphis, is known as the First Lady of Soul. One of American music's great treasures, Franklin has had one hit song after another, including "Respect." She has been nominated for more Grammy awards than any other female singer.

Nikki (Yolande Cornelia) Giovanni (1943–   ) is from Knoxville. She is best known for her popular children's poetry, as in her famous collection of poems, *Spin a Soft Black Song*. Her essays and brief life story are in her book *Gemini*.

Albert Gore Jr. (1948–   ) is known for his strong stand on the environment. Gore has been a U.S. senator and a member of Congress from Tennessee. He was elected vice president of the United States in 1992 and 1996.

Red Grooms (1937–   ), born in Nashville, is well known for his unusual sculptures. His artwork can be seen in modern-art museums across the United States.

Alex Haley (1921–1992), famous African-American author, hailed from Henning, Tennessee. It was on the front porch of his home in Henning that the young Haley first heard his family's fascinating stories about their past. Later, he used those stories to write *Roots*, an award-winning book and television miniseries that explored the overlooked history of African Americans. Haley's search for his roots led thousands of Americans to look for theirs.

W. C. Handy (1873–1958), who lived on Beale Street in Memphis, probably invented the blues. The blues is a mix of jazz and traditional work songs. Handy's songs include "Memphis Blues" and "Beale Street Blues." His work as a composer earned him the name Father of the Blues.

Sam Houston (1793–1863), though born in Virginia, lived with the Cherokee in Tennessee for several years. Like Davy Crockett, Houston lived a life of adventure. He fought with Andrew Jackson in the Creek War (1813–1814), served as a member of Congress from Tennessee and as governor of the state. Later, he moved to Texas, where he was one of the most important figures in Texas's fight for independence.

Cordell Hull (1871–1955), a native of Tennessee, is called the Father of the United Nations. Hull was secretary of state during World War II. After the war, he helped organize the United Nations as an international peacekeeping body.

Andrew Jackson

Cordell Hull

Andrew Jackson (1767–1845), the seventh president of the United States (1829–1837), served in the American Revolution at the age of 13.

He was also a hero of the War of 1812. During his long career, Jackson served as a judge, a U.S. representative, and a senator from Tennessee.

Andrew Johnson (1808–1875), who became the seventeenth president of the United States, came from a very poor Tennessee family. In 1864, he became Abraham Lincoln's running mate. The next year he became president when Lincoln was assassinated. In 1868, the House of Representatives impeached (brought charges against) him for his lenient attitude toward the South. The Senate refused to remove him from office by just one vote.

Estes Kefauver (1903–1963) of Tennessee was a member of the U.S. House of Representatives and then of the Senate. He became famous for his work on a Senate committee to fight organized crime. In 1956, he was the Democratic candidate for vice president on a ticket with Adlai Stevenson.

Martin Luther King Jr. (1929–1968) was a great American civil rights leader and the youngest person ever to win the Nobel Peace Prize. King was assassinated in Memphis in April 1968 while there to help the sanitation workers who were on strike.

Martin Luther King Jr.

Mary Love (famous in the 1860s), sometimes called the "Paul Revere of Tennessee," was a teenager when she made her famous ride. During the Civil War, Love hid in her clothing a message from General U. S. Grant to another Union general. She was caught by Confederate soldiers but refused to give them any information. The soldiers never found the message and let her go.

Satchel Paige (1906?–1982) was a star pitcher in the Negro leagues, the all-black professional baseball leagues. Paige played for both the Nashville Elite Giants and the Chattanooga Black Lookouts. After the integration of baseball, Paige joined the major leagues at age 42. He was the first member of the Negro leagues to become a member of the Baseball Hall of Fame.

Dolly Parton (1946–   ), a country music superstar, was born near Sevierville. Parton is famous for her singing and acting career. She is also part-owner of Dollywood, a huge musical theme park in Pigeon Forge, Tennessee.

James K. Polk (1795–1849) served as the eleventh U.S. president (1845–1849). Born in North Carolina, Polk was raised in Tennessee. He served as a member of the Tennessee legislature and the U.S. House of Representatives. He was also governor of Tennessee.

Elvis Presley (1935–1977), the "King of Rock 'n' Roll," was born in Mississippi but grew up and attended school in Memphis. Presley's first hits were recorded in Memphis at tiny Sun Studios. Elvis's mansion, Graceland, in Memphis, is filled with his gold records and glittering costumes and is one of the nation's most popular tourist attractions.

Ishmael Reed (1938–   ), born in Chattanooga, has used Tennessee in many of his writings. Reed is known for his poetry and fiction. Much of his writing is about the poor treatment of African Americans.

Wilma Rudolph (1940–1994) , a true Olympic champion, wore a leg brace as a child. Later, she went on to become a member of the Tigerbelles, the famous women's track team at Tennessee State University. In 1960, Rudolph became the first American woman to win three gold medals in track in the Olympics.

Wilma Rudolph

Clarence Saunders (1881–1953) of Memphis invented the first supermarket. Saunders's idea for the self-service food store changed the way Americans shopped. He called his store Piggly Wiggly after seeing a pig struggling to get under a fence.

Sequoyah (1760?–1843) invented an alphabet for the Cherokee language, thereby bringing reading and writing to his people, the Cherokee.

John Sevier (1745–1815) served as the first and only governor of the Republic of Franklin (1785–1788). In 1772, Sevier led a group of settlers (the Watauga Association) to start their own state. Franklin failed, and Sevier later became governor of Tennessee.

Nancy Ward (Nanye'-hi) (1738–1822), nicknamed Isistu-na-giska, or Cherokee Rose, was a leader of the Cherokee people. She believed in peace and often warned settlers about Cherokee attacks. When she married a white settler, Bryan Ward, she changed her first name to Nancy.

Ida B. Wells (1862–1931) of Memphis was a well-known early civil rights leader. After Wells was arrested for refusing to give up her seat in a railroad car to a group of white people, she sued the railroad. Although she lost, her case led many people to understand that segregation was unfair. Wells gained even greater fame as one of America's best-known black newspaper editors.

Oprah Winfrey (1954–   ) was born and raised in Tennessee and began her career at Nashville's Channel 5. Though Winfrey has starred in and produced films, her real fame has come as a popular television talk-show host. Today, she is one of the richest women in the United States.

Oprah Winfrey

Alvin C. York (1887–1964) is considered by many people to be the most famous hero of World War I. Born in the Cumberland Mountains of Tennessee, Sergeant York singlehandedly defeated a group of Germans at the Battle of the Argonne Forest (1918). For his bravery, he received the Congressional Medal of Honor, the highest award.

TOUR THE STATE

Andrew Johnson National Historic Site (Greeneville) The house Johnson lived in before he was president and his small tailor shop are interesting places to visit.

Davy Crockett Birthplace State Park (Limestone) A reconstruction of the tiny log cabin in which Davy Crockett was born stands where the original cabin once stood.

Rocky Mount (Piney Flats) This two-story log cabin, built in 1770, is the oldest original capital of a territory in the United States.

Cumberland Gap National Historic Park (Cumberland Gap) This 20,000-acre park is located in Tennessee, Virginia, and Kentucky, at the site where Daniel Boone found the Cumberland Gap, the passageway across the mountains to the West.

Great Smoky Mountains National Park (Great Smoky Mountains) Clingman's Dome, the highest point in Tennessee, and the Appalachian Trail make this park an awesome sight!

Norris Dam State Park (Norris) This park contains the Norris Dam, a product of the Tennessee Valley Authority (TVA), and the Lenoir Museum of interesting objects.

Museum of Appalachia (Norris) More than 25 reconstructed log cabins and thousands of real pioneer items can be found in this museum dedicated to the life and times of the Appalachian pioneer.

American Museum of Science and Energy (Oak Ridge) Hands-on displays and demonstrations teach visitors about the different kinds of energy.

Dollywood (Pigeon Forge) This large musical theme park, started by Dolly Parton, has thrilling rides, great entertainment, crafts, and shops.

Lost Sea Caverns (Sweetwater) Visitors can hike down to the world's largest underground lake (4½ acres) and ride in a glass-bottomed boat to see unusual sealife.

Sequoyah Birthplace Museum (Vonore) The life of Sequoyah, the inventor of the Cherokee alphabet, and the history of the Cherokee people are memorialized here.

Lookout Mountain (Chattanooga) Visitors can ride the world's steepest passenger railway a mile up to the top of the mountain, from where they can view seven states!

Tennessee Aquarium (Chattanooga) The aquatic exhibit is called the "world's first major freshwater life center" because it contains the 350 different kinds of fish found in the state.

Cherokee National Forest (Cleveland) This giant forest features scenic views, long hiking trails, and interesting wildlife.

Dunbar Cave State National Area (Clarksville) Nature walks, cave tours, and stories about the Native Americans who lived in these caves thousands of years ago are the attraction here.

Polk Ancestral Home (Columbia) Visit the historic home of one of America's least-known but hardest-working and most effective presidents.

The Old Stone Fort (Manchester) Once a mystery, this stone fort now stands in the middle of a state park. A museum gives information about the prehistoric Woodland Indians, who built the fort.

Opryland USA (Nashville) This musical theme park contains the Grand Ole Opry, the General Jackson Showboat, and television studios for two networks.

Nashville Toy Museum (Nashville) Teddy bears, dolls, dollhouses, toy cars, trucks, boats, planes, and two working model railroads make this a great place to visit.

Nashville Zoo (Nashville) Animals roam free in a beautiful country setting.

Cumberland Science Museum (Nashville) This hands-on museum has traveling science shows, displays about the environment, a planetarium, and live-animal demonstrations.

Music Row (Nashville) These streets in downtown Nashville contain museums of country music stars, recording studios, souvenir shops, and the Country Music Hall of Fame.

Capitol (Nashville) This beautiful building was completed in 1859, making it one of the oldest state capitols. President James K. Polk is buried inside.

Hermitage (near Nashville) Andrew Jackson, the seventh president, built and lived in this huge white home. The property also features its own church, log cabins, gardens, smokehouse, and tomb.

Shiloh National Military Park (Shiloh) The park is on the site of one of the bloodiest battles of the Civil War.

The Alex Haley House Museum (Henning) The porch of this house is where the young Haley heard stories about his family's history, which sparked the idea behind his famous book *Roots*. Each room in the museum tells a story about Haley's life.

Casey Jones Village (Jackson) A 15-minute video, an 1890s railroad car, and a full-size steam locomotive give visitors a chance to learn about the famous railroad engineer from American folklore Casey Jones.

Graceland (Memphis) The home of Elvis Presley, the "King of Rock and Roll," contains the fabulous souvenirs of the singer's lifetime.

National Civil Rights Museum (Memphis) The story of Martin Luther King Jr. and other civil rights leaders is told here, on the site of King's assassination.

Children's Museum of Memphis (Memphis) Young visitors can crawl through a tree house, climb an eight-story skyscraper, sit in a wheel-chair, "drive" a real car, and just have fun.

Peabody Hotel (Memphis) A duck parade twice a day from the lobby to the fountain of the hotel is one of the most popular sights in Memphis.

Chucalissa Indian Village (Memphis) A reconstructed Indian village at Memphis State University gives a very real picture of Native American life before the coming of white settlers.

Mississippi River Museum (Mud Island) This museum is a good way to learn about the history of the Mississippi River and its people.

Reelfoot Lake State Park (Tiptonville) Formed by a tremendous earthquake, this large park has boating, a wildlife refuge, a duck-calling contest, "eagle tours," and an arts and crafts festival in October.

FIND OUT MORE

Would you like to learn more about Tennessee? Look for the following titles in your library, bookstore, or video store. Your school librarian can help you find the CD-ROMs, videos, videodiscs, and computer software listed below.

BOOKS

Bertrand, Carolyn. *Nancy Ward, Cherokee*. New York: Dodd, Mead, and Co., 1975.

Bice, David A., and Jessie Shields Strickland. *Horizons of Tennessee*. Marceline, MO: Walsworth Publisher, 1989.

Carpenter, Allan. *The New Enchantment of America: Tennessee*. Chicago: Childrens Press, 1978.

Crawford, Charles W., Catherine Pickle, and Dennie L. Smith. *Dynamic Tennessee: Land, History, and Government*. Austin, TX: Steck-Vaughn, 1990.

McKissack, Patricia and Fredrick. *Tennessee Trailblazers*. Brentwood, TN: March Media, 1993.

WEBPAGES

http://www.state.tn.us

Frequently updated, this page is run by the Tennessee Board of Tourism.

http://www.inaugural.state.tn.us/hp/sundquist/tnintro.html

This is the official webpage of Tennessee's governor.

CD-ROMS

United States Geography: The Southeast, Clearvue/eav, Chicago, IL.

VIDEOS AND VIDEODISCS

The Geography of the Southeastern States. Society for Visual Education.

Looking for America: The Southeast. Clearvue/eav, Chicago, IL.

SOFTWARE

Great American States Race. Heartsoft, Tulsa, OK. This disk (PC or Mac) can be played at three levels of difficulty.

INDEX

Page numbers for illustrations are in boldface.